PRAISE FOR *A FIRE*

★ "Fies's personal, journalistic writing is more than match[ ]g, bright, and pleasantly old-school comics style . . . Sometimes incorporating photographs and often communicating emotion with color, he affectingly relates the grief, rage, and powerlessness of losing one's home and possessions; each time he remembers another thing he's lost—home videos he'd been meaning to digitize, for instance—the pain feels brand-new again. Inviting, empathy-driven, and ultimately hopeful in the face of hardship."
  —*Booklist*, **starred review**

★ "A vividly journalistic graphic narrative of resilience in the face of tragedy, an account of recent history that seems timely as ever . . . Drawings, words, and a few photos combine to convey the depth of a tragedy that would leave most people dumbstruck."
  —*Kirkus Reviews*, **starred review**

★ "'On Monday, my house disappeared,' begins this quietly devastating graphic memoir . . . Despite the pain he and his wife endure sifting through the ashes, Fies goes light on sentimentality, instead focusing on the realities of surviving the crisis and rebuilding literally from the ground up . . . Without pleading or preaching, this affecting record guides readers through the experience of enormous loss, then out through the other side."
  —*Publishers Weekly*, **starred review**

★ "Much like his Eisner Award–winning *Mom's Cancer*, this book is heartrending . . . In an era of increasing national disasters, this book will help teens understand the impact of tragic events. A must for most collections."
  —*School Library Journal*, **starred review**

"If only we could learn about every tragedy this way, instead of with screaming TV reporters and politicians arguing about whose fault it was."
  —*Advocate*

"*A Fire Story* is a perfect storm of a book, an individual graphic memoir that tells the larger story of a community, a comic that is the result of both long years of work and a viral internet sensation . . . It's a heartfelt, emotional read that has just as much historical and social worth as it does personal value, and a reminder of the best and worst parts of what people can be."
  —*A.V. Club*

"A moving and informative piece of journalism, one that relates not only the Fies couple's ordeal, but the experiences of others."
  —*Mercury News*

"*A Fire Story* has the feel of a touchstone book, something that will only (sadly) gain relevance as more and more of us are displaced by severe weather incidents that take our loved ones and our possessions, wiping away whole neighborhoods. It's exquisitely and subtly told."
  —**Cory Doctorow**, *Boing Boing*

"Brian Fies sat down with some Sharpies and some paper to process his pain the way he knows best. He began to draw. The result is *A Fire Story* . . . a webcomic that recounts the heart-wrenching devastation the California wildfires has wrought . . . Fies is a graphic novelist, one of the best in his field. A few years ago, when his mom was battling terminal cancer, he processed his grief by writing the comic *Mom's Cancer*. It won an Eisner Award, one of the comic world's highest achievements. Now he's had to do it all over again."
　　—CNN

"You can't get much more contemporary than a graphic novel about the wildfires in Northern California . . . Brian's skilled storytelling puts human faces on this life-changing environment."
　　—Diamond's Previews, Staff Picks

"As striking as it is detailed . . . Fies's attention to process—knowing the how, why, when, and where of very specific moments—gives the comic a sense of immediacy."
　　—Entertainment Weekly

"*A Fire Story* is urgent first-person journalism, encompassing the wider stories of fellow survivors and global climate change."
　　—Paul Gravett, *Bookseller*

"An effective snapshot of a broad disaster."
　　—io9

"Vibrant coloring and fascinating secondary stories create a gripping read that will attract graphic memoir fans and anyone seeking firsthand accounts of surviving a natural disaster."
　　—Library Journal

"Shares lesser-broadcast hardships as well as how quickly wildfire victims are expected to process a frenzied cycle of emotions . . . But a vulnerable Fies doesn't grieve alone—the careful accounting here culminates in what's better described as a work of comics journalism than it is autobiography . . . *A Fire Story* is a victim's testimony as well as a journalistic endeavor."
　　—Los Angeles Times

"A unique on-the-ground portrayal of the aftermath of the Tubbs Fire, which blazed through California's Napa and Sonoma counties in October of 2017 and turned his and his neighbors' lives upside down . . . In response, the cartoonist immediately started documenting the charred landscape, processing the wreckage the best way he knew how: through comics."
　　—Nation

"For award-winning writer and cartoonist Brian Fies, life will forever be divided into before and after October 9, 2017—the date Northern California's devastating Tubbs Fire devoured his home. In its aftermath, Fies felt compelled to process the trauma he experienced by drawing it. The resulting illustrations became popular online and are now a hardcover book, *A Fire Story*."
　　—PBS NewsHour

"Subtle and heart-wrenching."
　　—Press Democrat

A Fire Story

BRIAN FIES

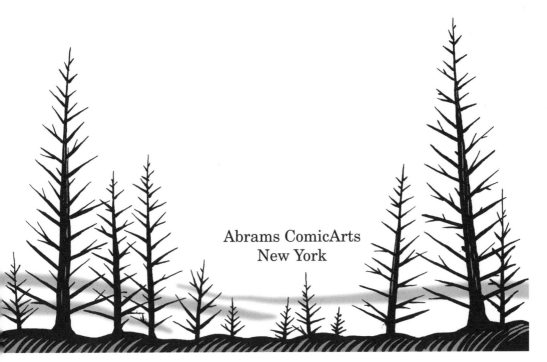

Abrams ComicArts
New York

Editor: Charles Kochman
Designer: Pamela Notarantonio
Managing Editor: Amy Vreeland
Production Manager: Alison Gervais

ISBN 978-1-4197-4682-6

Printed and bound in China
10 9 8 7 6 5 4 3 2 1

Abrams ComicArts books are available at special discounts when purchased in quantity
for premiums and promotions as well as fundraising or educational use. Special editions
can also be created to specification. For details, contact specialsales@abramsbooks.
com or the address below.

Abrams ComicArts® is a registered trademark of Harry N. Abrams, Inc.

ABRAMS The Art of Books
195 Broadway, New York, NY 10007
abramsbooks.com

To the memory of the forty-four

Acknowledgments

Special thanks to Mike, Dottie, Mary, Larry, Jerry, Sunny, and James for trusting me with their fire stories.

People who read early drafts of this book and gave me valuable feedback, not all of which I heeded, included Stephan Pastis, Richard Pini, Mike Peterson, MK Czerwiec, Don Rubin, Alexis Fajardo, and Jeff Kinney. Thank you, my friends. My best critiques came from Karen, Laura, and Robin Fies—eyewitnesses who vetoed surprisingly little.

Thanks to Charlie Kochman, the best kind of editor who makes me better without leaving fingerprints, and art director Pam Notarantonio, who made it easy. Thanks to the many people at Abrams who championed *A Fire Story*. Thanks also to the patient Stu Rees.

Thanks to Kelly Whalen, Farrin Abbott, and Gabe Meline at KQED for their expert storytelling and my astonishing Emmy.

Thanks to everyone who read the original webcomic or watched KQED's video. There'd be no book without you.

DISORIENTED AND SLEEPY, WE STUMBLED THROUGH OUR HOUSE WITH FLASHLIGHTS. I WAS **HYPERFOCUSED**, NOTICING WHATEVER FELL INTO MY BEAM BUT BLIND TO ANYTHING BEYOND IT.

I GRABBED "THIS" BUT LEFT "THAT," BECAUSE "THAT" WAS A FOOT TO ONE SIDE.

NEITHER OF US THOUGHT FOR A MOMENT THAT **ALL** OF IT MIGHT ACTUALLY BE GONE IN A FEW HOURS.

THIS WAS ONLY A DRILL. IT COULDN'T BE REAL.

CLOTHES I PACKED

TWO PAIRS OF SOCKS (SHORT AND LONG)

STRIPED T-SHIRT

FLANNEL SHIRT

SWEATSHIRT

TOILETRY BAG

TWO TIGHTY-WHITEYS

PLUS THE JEANS, SHIRT, JACKET,
AND SANDALS I THREW ON

STUFF WE GRABBED

OUR DOG, RILEY

OUR CAT, AMBER

PHOTO ALBUMS

A FEW FRAMED PHOTOS AND ART

ONE COPY OF EACH OF MY BOOKS,
ENGLISH AND FOREIGN (I MISSED A FEW)

SOME JEWELRY

DRAWER OF IMPORTANT PAPERS

COMPUTER BACKUP AND USB DRIVES

WALLET, PURSE, AND CELL PHONES

OUR DAUGHTERS' BEST STUFFED
BUDDIES FROM INFANCY, BOO BEAR
AND PIGLET

WTF?

4

7

8

WE DIDN'T KNOW ANY OF THAT WHEN WE LEFT HOME, FULLY EXPECTING TO RETURN VERY SOON. THE IDEA OF THAT DISTANT GLOW IN THE SKY ACTUALLY REACHING US WAS LUDICROUS.

WHERE SHOULD WE GO?

YOUR OFFICE.

KAREN IS DIRECTOR OF SONOMA COUNTY HUMAN SERVICES. HER OFFICE HAS A BACKUP GENERATOR, TELEPHONES, INTERNET, AND A SODA MACHINE. IT'S ALSO ONLY A FEW MILES FROM OUR HOUSE. WE COULD HOLE UP THERE.

BESIDES, KAREN WAS PART OF THE COUNTY EMERGENCY RESPONSE TEAM. SHE HAD TO HELP IMPLEMENT THE MAJOR DISASTER PLAN.

13

MY PATH TOOK ME OVER HIGHWAY 101, AN ARTERY LINKING LOS ANGELES AND OREGON.

SIX LANES, EMPTY. I'D NEVER SEEN IT EMPTY BEFORE.

THE FIRE HAD JUMPED THE FREEWAY A COUPLE OF MILES SOUTH, BUT I DIDN'T KNOW THAT YET.

THE SUN WAS A DIM ORANGE DISK BEHIND A SALMON-GRAY CURTAIN OF SMOKE.

I INHALED MY NEIGHBORS' LIVES.

I KEPT WAITING FOR SOMEBODY TO STOP ME, BUT NO ONE DID.

A FIREHOSE, SPLIT AND MELTED ON THE STREET—A VALIANT LAST STAND ROUTED INTO RETREAT.

A FALLEN HOOP THAT A BOY LOBBED BASKETBALLS AT FOR HOURS EVERY EVENING AFTER DINNER.

THE STEEL POSTS OF MAILBOXES, TWISTED AND STRETCHED LIKE HOT SUMMER TAFFY.

TOMMY THE COP BOUGHT A HOUSE NEXT TO ONE HE'D BEEN RENTING. HIS FAMILY MOVED IN LAST MONTH.

LOU HAD A MODEL TRAIN LAYOUT TAKING UP HALF HIS GARAGE THAT WAS ALREADY DECORATED FOR CHRISTMAS.

NONNA TONI ALWAYS BAKED FOCACCIA FOR BLOCK PARTIES, DESPITE BEING TOO INFIRM TO ATTEND HERSELF.

BOB AND ROBYN LEFT FOR ROME TWO DAYS AGO. THEIR CAR BLED MOLTEN ALUMINUM INTO THE GUTTER.

I LOOKED DOWN MY STREET, STUPIDLY HOPING TO SEE A MIRACLE.

20

I TRIED TO CALL A NEIGHBOR TO TELL HER, TOO, BUT RECEPTION WAS BAD AND I ENDED UP SHOUTING AT HER.

YOUR HOUSE IS GONE! IT'S ALL GONE!

NO, GONE!

IT WOULD HAVE ALMOST BEEN FUNNY IF I WEREN'T RUINING HER LIFE.

I TOOK A FEW PHOTOS BUT DIDN'T LINGER.

SPOTS WERE STILL BURNING, AND I SUDDENLY FELT EXPOSED AND VULNERABLE.

24

I DIDN'T COME FROM THAT WAY, BUT THEY'RE PROBABLY FINE.

THANK GOD!

A WEEK LATER I LEARNED I WAS WRONG. THEIR HOME HAD BURNED DOWN, TOO.

I'LL ALWAYS FEEL A TWINGE OF GUILT FOR RAISING HOPES THAT WERE DASHED A FEW MINUTES LATER.

KAREN WAS A HERO THE REST OF THE DAY. WITH NINE-TENTHS OF HER STAFF OUT, SHE LED A TEAM THAT IMPROVISED AND PROBLEM-SOLVED. IT WAS IMPRESSIVE.

OUR GIRLS HAVE BEEN ON THEIR OWN FOR YEARS, BUT OUR HOME WAS THEIRS, TOO. MOST OF THEIR CHILDHOOD VANISHED IN A NIGHT. THEY WERE HURTING THE SAME AS WE WERE, BUT BEING STRONG FOR US.

THIS WAS THE FIRST TIME IN OUR CHILDREN'S LIVES WE REALLY NEEDED THEIR HELP. IT PROBABLY WON'T BE THE LAST TIME FOR **THAT**, EITHER.

KAREN AND I WERE PRACTICALLY NEWLYWEDS THREE DECADES AGO, WHEN WE MOVED TO MY HOMETOWN OF SANTA ROSA AND RENTED A DUPLEX.

A COUPLE OF YEARS LATER, WE BOUGHT OUR FIRST HOUSE IN COFFEY PARK. I'LL NEVER FORGET KAREN TELLING ME SHE WAS EXPECTING AS WE STOOD IN THAT DRIVEWAY.

WE MADE IT THROUGH HER DIFFICULT PREGNANCY WHILE PUTTING UP A FENCE, BUILDING A DECK, PLANTING SOD, AND DOING THE MILLION CHORES IT TAKES TO SET UP A HOUSEHOLD. OUR FAMILY LIVED IN THAT LITTLE HOME UNTIL OUR GIRLS ENTERED SIXTH GRADE, WHEN WE MOVED TO A LARGER HOUSE SO THEY COULD STAY IN THEIR SCHOOL DISTRICT AND HAVE THEIR OWN ROOMS.

THE FIRESTORM DESTROYED ALL THREE PLACES, MILES APART FROM ONE ANOTHER—THE DUPLEX, THE COFFEY PARK HOUSE, AND THE HOUSE WE FLED FROM THAT NIGHT. NEARLY EVERYWHERE I'D LIVED AS A MARRIED ADULT. EVERY HOME OUR DAUGHTERS HAD KNOWN UNTIL THEY LEFT FOR COLLEGE.

THAT'S A LOT OF HISTORY TO LOSE IN ONE BLOW.

IN QUIET MOMENTS, WE INVENTORIED LOST TREASURES, EACH A SHARP STAB TO THE HEART. WE DIDN'T SAVE THE **WRONG** STUFF, LIKE THE PEOPLE WHO RISK THEIR LIVES FOR A JAR OF PICKLES. WE JUST DIDN'T SAVE **ENOUGH** OF IT.

THINGS I WILL NEVER SEE AGAIN

MY GRANDMA'S DEPRESSION-ERA GLASS CANDY JAR

MY GRANDPA'S WORLD WAR II FIELD CAP

OUR ANTIQUE PHONOGRAPH

CHILD-MADE CHRISTMAS ORNAMENTS

A TIME CAPSULE OF NEWSPAPERS AND MAGAZINES I BOUGHT THE DAY MY GIRLS WERE BORN

AN APOLLO SPACECRAFT MODEL SIGNED BY ASTRONAUT DICK GORDON, WHO DIED A MONTH AFTER THE FIRE

A LITTLE BOOK MY FRIEND JIM AND I WROTE IN EIGHTH GRADE, WHICH HE ENTRUSTED TO ME WHEN HE DIED TWENTY YEARS AGO

MY GREAT-GRANDMOTHER'S SET OF THE 1892 ENCYCLOPEDIA BRITANNICA

MY MOM'S DIAMOND EARRINGS WE PLANNED TO RE-SET AND GIVE TO OUR GIRLS ON THEIR NEXT BIRTHDAY

A SERIES OF FAMILY PICTURES TAKEN BY CRAMMING ALL OF US INTO A PHOTO BOOTH AT THE COUNTY FAIR EVERY SUMMER FOR TWENTY YEARS

EVERYTHING I EVER DREW OR PAINTED OR MADE

EVERYTHING ELSE.

ON TUESDAY, I BOUGHT SHOES FOR WALKING AND BOOTS FOR DIGGING.

I SAW THINGS I'D NEEDED TWO DAYS EARLIER—FURNACE FILTERS, PRINTER INK, LIGHTBULBS— AND REALIZED I DIDN'T ANYMORE.

IT'S UNNERVING TO NEED BOTH **EVERYTHING** AND **NOTHING**.

YOU CAN TELL AT A GLANCE IF A SHOPPER HAS LOST EVERYTHING THEY OWN.

UNDERWEAR, SOCKS, SHOES, BOTTLED WATER, TOOTHBRUSH AND TOOTHPASTE, ONE LIGHT SHIRT, ONE HEAVY SHIRT.

YOU LOOK INTO THEIR CART. THEY LOOK INTO YOURS. SOMETIMES IT SPARKS A CONVERSATION.

USUALLY A NOD.

FINDING A **CAPTAIN AMERICA** T-SHIRT TOUCHED OFF THE **SECOND** TIME I TEARED UP SINCE THE FIRE. I DON'T KNOW WHY.

BECAUSE ALL I HAD TO SHOW FOR A LIFETIME OF READING, COLLECTING, LOVING, AND MAKING COMICS WAS ASH? BECAUSE CAPTAIN AMERICA ALWAYS DOES THE RIGHT THING FOR THE RIGHT REASON AND NEVER GIVES UP?

SOMETHING ABOUT THAT ICONOGRAPHY STIRRED DEEP AND STRONG FEELINGS.

I JUST WISH THEY'D HAD ONE IN MY SIZE.

I STILL CARRY OUR GARAGE DOOR OPENER IN THE CAR.

I PRESSED THE BUTTON ONCE.

NOTHING HAPPENED.

MY KEY RING HAS FIVE KEYS. THREE OF THEM DON'T DO ANYTHING ANYMORE.

Front door

Mailbox melted on sidewalk

Car incinerated in garage

I WONDER HOW LONG IT'LL BE BEFORE I CAN BEAR TO TAKE THEM OFF.

MIKE'S FIRE STORY

OTHER PEOPLE HAVE THEIR OWN FIRE STORIES TO TELL. MICHAEL W. HARKINS IS A JOURNALIST, MEDIA CONSULTANT, AND AUTHOR OF THE BOOK *MOVE TO FIRE*. HIS WIFE, ELIZABETH, IS AN ATTORNEY. THEY LIVED IN A SMALL NEIGHBORHOOD NEAR COFFEY PARK.

I was awake. It was probably 1:30 in the morning, and I've had this habit for decades, before turning off the lights, of channel-surfing to different news stations.

Only one news station had a live remote reporting on the fires. I was watching it, and Elizabeth woke up and came down the hall and said, "What's going on?" I pointed at the TV and said, "This."

As we watched, they said the fire had just jumped 101. We said, "Huh." Then the power went out, and we said, "OK, time to pack." We made a major error in judgment, which I think many people did; we packed thinking we'd be back in a day or so.

Our neighbor Maria is handicapped, so I went outside to check on her. Maria was thinking she might actually try to stay. We just couldn't sort out the situation because we had no idea about the enormity of what was happening. We couldn't see anything. But the sky got oranger and oranger.

I went inside and said, "Elizabeth, you have to go." She said, "You're coming with me." I said, "I can't. I have to make sure Maria's out of here." Elizabeth looked at me and said, "You're going to be right behind me, right?" I said "Yes," and I meant that. So Elizabeth left.

Maria's housemate, Dane, and I got Maria into a van. They got out all right. By then the fire was coming across a field to the first house in our neighborhood. Our neighbor Matt had a power washer and a generator, and was trying to keep the flames back. I took my hose over to his house and hooked it up.

We could feel the superheated air. After a while another neighbor came over and said, "We have to go." Matt got his stuff together and left. I went back to my house and reconnected the hose. Pretty soon it was just me.

I turned on the hose at the front of the house and another at the back, and left them on. Then, for the rest of the night, I ran from front to back, and across the street and down the block, to stomp out little fires as they started.

Embers on roofs were not a problem. They hit the asphalt shingles; they were featherweight and glowing, but their conductivity wasn't such that they could get through the shingles. What happened was, embers would float down and land on vegetation: dry grass and leaves. They'd be blown under trees and bushes, and fires would flare up.

The turning point of the night was when the fire flanked me. My neighbor Tony's son had a car parked in his driveway with a car cover on, and I heard this *fwoomp* to my left, which was the entire car cover going up at once. That surprised me. That's the first time during the night I thought, "You need to be more aware! You *think* you're aware, but you are not in charge."

As the fire spread behind me from places I couldn't see, there would be an explosion followed by a kind of jet stream of glowing golden particles. Like a special effect from a fantasy film.

There was one in particular that I looked up and remember thinking that it was, in the weirdest way, beautiful. Mesmerizing. I couldn't *not* watch it. Like a golden Milky Way. Then I realized that I should actually watch where they landed! I could see them drop down, and knew I had to note where they went. After a while it happened so much I couldn't note them anymore.

When a car explodes, first the windows blow out. Then oil and fluids in the engine go. Tires go next. But the big one is the gas tank. I was fifteen feet away and it went with a *boom!*

So Tony's kid's car goes up. His garage is starting to go, his house is going to go. I knew if the fire came around the front and turned the corner toward my house, it was going to be extremely difficult for me to do any more.

One of the reasons I stayed is I had just seen my dad in July. I went to Ireland; he and his wife, Marian, built a cottage about two miles from where he was born. I went for his ninetieth birthday, and every time I see him I hear stories I'd never heard before . . .

He was once out boating on Lake Michigan. There was a huge storm. Something had come apart on the boat and he had to crawl out and up to repair the thing, or die. The man is so capable. In his life he's been a karate instructor. He's been an engineer. He's been an officer in the Coast Guard Reserve and a ski patrol guy. And he came back into the boat looking like hell, but fine. He said, "I knew if I could get to it, I could fix it." That was in my mind. I thought, "If I can just maintain this, I can make it."

MIKE FOUGHT THE FIRE ALONE WITH A GARDEN HOSE FROM ABOUT 4 TO 7 A.M.

I'm a Buddhist, raised Catholic. I became a Buddhist as a teenager after martial arts introduced me to Zen and Buddhism in grammar school. People say Buddhism is the religion that has no god. The more appropriate modern response is, "If there is a god, it doesn't matter. I still try to live my life right, in harmony with the universe." But that night, when I decided to stay, I did say out loud to the universe, "You've gotta give me this!"

Whatever I was talking to replied, "I'll give you a few hours. We'll see what happens."

Explosions were constant. I haven't been in a war but I was in the Army, with plenty of training exercises. They sounded like different calibers going off, all night long.

The fire's coming around. Superheated air is so hot! Within a minute, it started to blister my skin. Embers came down and burned through my shirt—I still have the shirt, Elizabeth kept it for me. I backed off and knew (a) I didn't have enough water to reach it, and (b) I couldn't get any closer. As I watched, the walls of my house started to bubble. And I thought, "That's it. My house is done." Then I heard a power saw.

Suddenly he's just there: a firefighter from Berkeley Engine 6, next to me with a real hose. He barely glances at me, just walks a little closer than I can get, and says as he's walking by, "Let's see if we can save your house."

He hits it with this beautiful stream of water I would have given my leg for earlier in the evening. He's hitting my house, he's hitting Tony's house. He worked on it for about a minute. We both saw: the windows had blown out of my house. We could see flames inside coming up the hallway. And through the foundation vents, we could look down there and see flames under the house.

He said, "I don't think we can save this." I said, "I know."

The firefighter looked right at me and said, "I'm sorry I couldn't save your house."

I'm thinking, "With all the shit you have to do, you're taking a moment to look at me and convey, 'I know you're losing everything and I'm really sorry.'" It's one of the most humanitarian moments of my life. Then he and his crew saved the rest of my neighborhood.

Mike took this final photo of his home.

MIKE BEGAN HIS CAREER IN MUSIC AS A ROADIE FOR THE BAND JOURNEY IN 1976, BEFORE THEY BECAME FAMOUS.

Journey, in their early days, were kind of an extended jam band, perfect for a young man who plays guitar to become enamored with. As Journey got big, they became pioneers in the large-screen projection video that's now part of every big concert. They formed their own production company called Nocturne to do those shows. I'd been a film and video major before I left art school, so I joined Nocturne and worked with all these bands: Santana, Prince, the Police, Springsteen.

My last gig was road manager for Michael Jackson's *Bad* tour in Japan and Australia in 1987. I dealt with the guest lists, everybody from Cheryl Tiegs to Gregory Peck. One of the most memorable moments of my rock-and-roll career was shooting the breeze with Gregory Peck at a stadium in Tokyo.

I had kept all the lists I'd made of famous people calling, all the visitor passes and tour passes. Documents from the venues. Things that nobody in the world had but me. I lost all my Michael Jackson stuff. All my Journey stuff. All these things I'd made an effort to keep, not just because they were memorabilia but because they meant so much to me. ■ The fire took them all.

SONOMA COUNTY HAS A **MEDITERRANEAN** CLIMATE. MILD WEATHER, WET WINTERS, DRY SUMMERS AND AUTUMNS.

IT REMINDED NINETEENTH-CENTURY ITALIAN IMMIGRANTS OF HOME.

THE TUSCAN SETTLERS' LEGACY SURVIVES IN THE NAMES OF STREETS AND PARKS, THE REGION'S WORLD-CLASS VINEYARDS, AND A FEW STONE HOTELS AND HOP KILNS THAT SURVIVED THE 1906 EARTHQUAKE.

YEARS OF DROUGHT WEAKENED AND DRIED THE NATIVE OAK TREES, WHICH WERE ALREADY PLAGUED BY SUDDEN OAK DEATH SYNDROME.

LAST YEAR'S DROUGHT-BUSTING RAINS WERE HEAVIER THAN AVERAGE, WHICH PARADOXICALLY MADE THE PROSPECTS FOR DEVASTATING FIRE **WORSE.**

ONE SEASON'S DOWNPOURS DIDN'T HELP THE TREES MUCH, BUT THEY FED A BUMPER CROP OF **GRASSES** THAT, HALF A YEAR LATER, DRIED INTO A GOLDEN CARPET OF KINDLING.

NOBODY COULD BLAME THIS **PARTICULAR** FIRE ON **CLIMATE CHANGE.** BUT AS HEAT BUILDS UP IN THE AIR AND OCEANS, AND HISTORIC WEATHER PATTERNS SHIFT, DISASTERS LIKE THESE WILL BECOME MORE COMMON.

THE NORTHERN CALIFORNIA WILDFIRES COMPRISED SEVERAL SEPARATE BLAZES—INCLUDING THE TUBBS, NUNS, ATLAS, POCKET, SULPHUR, CASCADE, AND REDWOOD VALLEY FIRES—THAT BEGAN OCTOBER 8 AND 9, 2017, THEN BURNED IN EIGHT COUNTIES OVER THE NEXT TWO WEEKS. THEY DESTROYED ABOUT 8,900 STRUCTURES, INCLUDING MORE THAN 6,200 HOMES. FORTY-FOUR PEOPLE DIED.

SCHOOLS, SHOPS, AND ROADS STAYED CLOSED. POWER AND GAS WERE TURNED OFF. THOUSANDS WERE EVACUATED, WITH NOWHERE PARTICULAR TO GO. THOUSANDS MORE LINGERED ANXIOUSLY, CARS PACKED AND READY TO FLEE THE METASTASIZING DISASTER.

WE ARE HERE.

FIRES LICKED AT THE EDGES OF TOWNS FOR DAYS, WHILE SMOKE AND ASH BLOTTED THE SKY.

KAREN STAYED IN CRISIS MODE, WHILE HER STAFF—MANY OF WHOM HAD LOST THEIR HOMES, TOO— TRICKLED IN THROUGH THE WEEK.

MEANWHILE, I BEGAN MAKING CALLS.

A DAY IN THE NEW LIFE

THE COUNTY OF SONOMA SET UP A LOCAL ASSISTANCE CENTER DOWNTOWN THAT SERVED THOUSANDS WHO LOST BIRTH CERTIFICATES, MARRIAGE LICENSES, DRIVER'S LICENSES, PROPERTY RECORDS, UTILITY BILLS, AND OTHER VITAL RECORDS. BY MOST ACCOUNTS THEY DID A GOOD JOB.

THE FEDERAL EMERGENCY MANAGEMENT AGENCY (FEMA) CAME TO TOWN, REASSURINGLY COMPETENT AND CARING.

THE U.S. NATIONAL OCEANOGRAPHIC AND ATMOSPHERIC ADMINISTRATION (NOAA) CALLED 2017 "A HISTORIC YEAR OF WEATHER AND CLIMATE DISASTERS" FOR THE UNITED STATES. FIFTY-SEVEN MAJOR DISASTERS WERE DECLARED THROUGHOUT THE YEAR, WITH SIXTEEN OF THEM CAUSING MORE THAN $1 BILLION IN DAMAGE.

Northern California Firestorm, October

Hurricane Maria, September

Thomas Fire, December

Hurricane Harvey, August

Hurricane Irma, August

THE NATION'S ABILITY TO COPE WITH CRISES WAS STRETCHED THIN.

FEMA'S CRITICAL CONCERN WAS **HOUSING:** RENTALS, TRAILERS, HOTEL VOUCHERS. BECAUSE OUR DAUGHTERS TOOK US IN, FEMA DIDN'T NEED TO DO ANYTHING FOR US. BUT OTHER GROUPS FUNNELED CHARITABLE GIVING INTO CASH THAT WE COULD USE.

A-F

G-L

HEY, I GOT MY CHECK!

Neighbor from two blocks over

50

A VETERINARY OFFICE GAVE US A CASE OF PRESCRIPTION DOG FOOD.

A SYNDICATED CARTOONIST I'VE NEVER MET MAILED ME PENS AND PENCILS. OTHER CARTOONISTS SENT ART, BOOKS, EVEN MONEY.

A LOCAL GOVERNMENT-BACKED ARTS GROUP, CREATIVE SONOMA, GAVE ME CASH TOWARD NEW ART EQUIPMENT AND MATERIALS.

A STATIONER SENT US HOME WITH TWO BAGS OF FREE OFFICE SUPPLIES.

BOY SCOUT TROOPS AND OTHERS BUILT SIFTING SCREENS BY THE HUNDREDS.

SCHOOLKIDS IN OCEANSIDE, NEW YORK, HAND-PAINTED WOODEN STARS THAT HUNG IN OUR BURNED TREES LIKE ORNAMENTS.

FOOD AND CLOTHES BANKS POPPED UP IN VACANT STOREFRONTS.

MANY STORES OFFERED DISCOUNTS TO FIRE VICTIMS, NO PROOF REQUIRED.

PEOPLE WERE ALSO OPPORTUNISTIC AND CRUEL.

LOOTERS AND METAL THIEVES PICKED THROUGH PROPERTY THAT WAS OFF-LIMITS TO EVEN THOSE OF US WHO LIVED THERE.

SHERIFF'S DEPUTIES, CALIFORNIA HIGHWAY PATROL, AND NATIONAL GUARD TROOPS BLOCKED ROUTES INTO BURNED AREAS. ENTIRE SWATHS OF THE COUNTY—INCLUDING OUR NEIGHBORHOOD—WERE CORDONED OFF.

IT'S NOT RIGHT.

WE ALREADY KNEW THERE WAS LITTLE TO GO BACK TO, BUT THE IDEA OF LOOTERS SCAVENGING THROUGH OUR RUINS BEFORE WE HAD A CHANCE TO WAS MADDENING. OBSCENE.

STILL, SOMEDAY THEY'D LET US RETURN HOME. WHEN THEY DID, WE WERE GOING TO NEED **TOOLS.**

SEEING A WALL OF **HAMMERS** SET OFF THE **THIRD** TIME I'D TEARED UP SINCE THE FIRE.

WHAT PATHETIC EXCUSE OF A MAN DOESN'T EVEN OWN A DAMN HAMMER?

I CHOSE ONE THAT FELT RIGHT.

DOTTIE'S FIRE STORY

DOROTHY HUGHES LIVED IN JOURNEY'S END, A MOBILE HOME PARK OCCUPIED BY LOW-INCOME SENIORS. IT WAS NEXT TO HIGHWAY 101, JUST WEST OF THE FOUNTAINGROVE NEIGHBORHOOD. ONLY FORTY-FOUR OF ITS 160 HOMES SURVIVED. DOTTIE WAS EIGHTY-ONE AT THE TIME OF THE FIRE.

My niece called me. She said, "Auntie, if you're on any kind of medication, grab your medications and come up to my house." She didn't say "fire," she just said, "Get up to my house." I could tell by the tone of her voice to listen to her.

I grabbed some insurance papers and things like that, and got in my car. As I was driving out, the wind was blowing the fire across the street from Fountaingrove.

I knew it was going to hit Journey's End. My street had newer mobile homes, but it hit the older ones first. I know how mobile courts go. If one starts, they all go.

I got to my niece's house, but they were in jeopardy, too. We drove to one evacuation center, bumper to bumper, but people came out into the street and said, "Turn around, they're full." So we went to the Veterans' Memorial Building.

I saw a man from Journey's End named John. He was with his little dog, and he was barefoot. So I took off my socks and went over and said, "Put these on to keep your feet warm and I'll go get you a bottle of water." About that time, they told him he had to leave because of his dog, which was all he had in the world. I couldn't find him after that.

We stayed there all night long. Finally my son wanted to go see if my place was still standing. Well, they wouldn't even let us go down the street. And I didn't really want to see, to tell you the truth. I was scared.

My son said, "Let's sneak in through the Kaiser hospital next door," because my house backs right up against it. So we went around and through Kaiser. And my house was still standing! When the firemen were fighting to save the hospital they hosed down my whole street. That's why those forty-four homes survived.

I just thanked God for blessing us. But it's a Catch-22, since Journey's End is too unsafe to live in, but insurance won't pay for the houses because they're still standing.

The Journey's End owners locked us out. I was picketing. "Let us go home!" "We're too old to start over!" I was in the newspapers. That's not like me, I don't do those things! But it's like we've fallen through the cracks. You hear about Fountaingrove and Coffey Park, but Journey's End is the truly forgotten one.

Some people have given up and moved to Sacramento because they couldn't afford to stay here. That hurts us more, because it means fewer people are here fighting to get back what's ours.

At the beginning, they said it was feasible to open up the forty-four houses and let us return. But now they're saying no, it's too hard to get new utilities in there for us. But they're going to have to put in utilities for whatever replaces us, so that doesn't add up to me.

I hate to give up hope, but it doesn't look good at all. I try very hard not to think about it because I get so upset about never, ever being able to live there again.

DOTTIE'S HUSBAND, ALBERT, DIED IN FEBRUARY 2017.

Every night I wake up worrying about something. I think the hardest part is not having my husband with me. I just miss him. I feel like he'd have some ideas of what to do or where to go. I'm doing the best I can. Every day I'm going someplace, trying to figure out what to do or where to get help. I'm thankful for any help I get, but if I had him it would be so much easier.

But I don't know if he could have lived through what I've been through. Sometimes women are stronger when it comes to that, you know.

We were together fifty-nine years. He wanted so much to make it to sixty.

I love my mobile, but it's too old to be moved. It's a really nice double-wide. I had a nice patio, a nice yard. I was very comfortable. We lived there twenty-nine years and I thought it was where my life would come to an end.

I have a key to the gate now. I guess I think I'm still going to be able to move back sometime, because I fill up jugs and take them over there to water my flowers.

DOTTIE LIVED IN A FEMA-SUBSIDIZED MOTEL ROOM, ACROSS THE FREEWAY FROM HER FORMER HOME, FOR EIGHT MONTHS.

I managed with a little refrigerator and a toaster oven. I washed dishes, sometimes in the little sink and sometimes in the bathtub. I tried to go to the grocery store to get my mind off things. It was just horrible living that way.

I get supplements because I know I'm not eating like I should be. We eat out a lot, but I'm Italian, so I love to cook. I say I have pasta withdrawal. That's the one thing I can't do without.

IN JUNE 2018, DOTTIE MOVED INTO A SMALL APARTMENT PROVIDED BY THE NON-PROFIT BURBANK HOUSING.

From what I hear I'm very lucky to get a place, because most of the Journey's End people keep getting refusal letters. I wasn't happy about going there, but I know I'm blessed to have a place because so many don't. It's just so far from what I used to have.

I just hope that God blesses me with a little more time on this Earth to be happy and not sad every day, and not wake up in the middle of the night wondering what's going to happen tomorrow. It's been hell since the fire. ■

IMAGINE THE IMPACT THAT TEN THOUSAND PEOPLE INSTANTLY HOMELESS, AND THOUSANDS MORE INSTANTLY JOBLESS, HAVE ON A LOCAL ECONOMY.

THE RICH WERE FINE. THEIR INSURERS SNAPPED UP EVERY AVAILABLE VACANCY AND BID UP RENTS THAT FORCED THE LESS WELL-OFF TO PAY INFLATED RATES FOR SHACKS FORTY MILES AWAY.

HOMEOWNERS ALREADY PLANNING TO SELL MADE QUICK DEALS AT PEAK PRICES.

RENTERS WERE EVICTED BY LANDLORDS WHO'D LOST THEIR OWN HOMES AND DESPERATELY NEEDED A ROOF OF THEIR OWN.

LAWS WERE QUICKLY PASSED FORBIDDING RENT HIKES MORE THAN 10 PERCENT OVER PRE-FIRE PRICES, BUT LOOPHOLES AND SHARKS ABOUNDED.

A DAY IN THE NEW LIFE

WITH NO MAILBOXES TO BE DELIVERED TO, OUR MAIL FLOATED THROUGH THE POSTAL SYSTEM. WE WAITED IN LONG LINES AT ONE POST OFFICE, ONLY TO BE TOLD OUR MAIL WAS SENT TO ANOTHER.

WRITE YOUR ADDRESS ON THIS CARD AND WAIT UNTIL IT'S CALLED!

WRITE YOUR ADDRESS ON THIS CARD AND WAIT UNTIL IT'S CALLED!

WHAT A CRUMMY SYSTEM!

I'VE BEEN HERE FOR AN HOUR!

HEY, HONEY. I BROUGHT YOU A SANDWICH.

THANKS, BABE! I HAVEN'T EATEN SINCE YESTERDAY.

A MINUTE AGO, THIS POSTAL WORKER WAS A FRUSTRATING BUREAUCRATIC ROADBLOCK.

4404 OLD REDWOOD HIGHWAY?

SUDDENLY HE WAS ONE OF US, HANDLING A CRISIS HE WAS NEVER PREPARED FOR AS BEST HE COULD.

I SPENT THE NEXT THREE DAYS COPYING AND PASTING **THOUSANDS** OF INDIVIDUAL FILES FROM THE BACKUP TO MY NEW HARD DRIVE. BUT AT LEAST I STILL HAD THEM.

THE ELECTRONS CLINGING TO THAT FRAGILE MAGNETIC DISC WERE NEARLY ALL THAT REMAINED OF THE PHOTOS I'D TAKEN, THE ARTICLES I'D WRITTEN, THE BOOKS I'D DONE, THE BOOKS I PLANNED TO DO, AND EVERYTHING ELSE I'D EVER CREATED.

I NEVER TRUSTED CLOUD STORAGE. BUT IF I HADN'T GRABBED THAT BACKUP THE NIGHT OF THE FIRE, I'D HAVE LOST IT ALL.

I'M A CONVERT TO THE CLOUD.

TWO OF THEM, CALLED "SOCO ALERT" AND "NIXLE," REACHED TELEPHONE LANDLINES AND PEOPLE WHO SIGNED UP IN ADVANCE TO GET TEXT MESSAGES.

NOT MANY PEOPLE GOT THOSE ALERTS.

THE THIRD IS THE FAMILIAR "EMERGENCY ALERT SYSTEM" ON TV AND RADIO. THE FOURTH, "WIRELESS EMERGENCY ALERT" (WEA), PUSHES ALARMS TO CELL PHONES.

THOSE TWO SYSTEMS **WEREN'T USED** THE NIGHT OF THE FIRE.

DISASTER OFFICIALS LATER SAID THEY DIDN'T WANT TO CAUSE WIDESPREAD PANIC THAT MIGHT HAVE GRIDLOCKED STREETS AND CAUSED MORE DEATHS. SO THEY STAYED SILENT INSTEAD.

THERE'S A BONE-CHILLING LOGIC TO SACRIFICING THE LIVES OF **SOME** TO POSSIBLY SAVE THE LIVES OF A FEW **MORE**. STILL . . .

REGARDLESS—IF YOU WON'T PUSH THE BIG RED BUTTON WHEN STORMFRONTS OF FLAME ARE OBLITERATING THOUSANDS OF HOMES, WHAT'S THE POINT OF HAVING ONE?

VERY LARGE STARS DIE IN A SUPERNOVA, AN EXPLOSION OF LIGHT AND HEAT THAT BRIEFLY BRIGHTENS AN ENTIRE GALAXY.

THEIR CORES COLLAPSE TO A POINT, CREATING A SPHERE OF SPACE WHERE GRAVITY IS SO STRONG NOT EVEN LIGHT CAN ESCAPE: A **BLACK HOLE**.

THE FIRE IS OUR BLACK HOLE.

WE ORBIT THE DARK VOIDS WHERE OUR HOMES USED TO BE, BOUND BY INVISIBLE CABLES ANCHORED TO GHOSTS.

OLD NEIGHBORS MEET IN THE LOCAL GROCERY STORE EVEN THOUGH WE ALL NOW LIVE TWENTY MILES AWAY. WE SEE EACH OTHER EATING LUNCH IN OUR CARS, PARKED AT OUR FORMER CURBS. NO EXPLANATION NEEDED; WE FEEL THE SAME PULL.

MARY & LARRY'S FIRE STORY

LARRY TERBUSH IS RETIRED FROM A THIRTY-FIVE-YEAR CAREER WITH THE FBI. HIS WIFE, MARY, BEGAN HER CAREER AS FBI CLERICAL STAFF, WHERE SHE MET LARRY, AND RECENTLY RETIRED FROM HER JOB AS A HEALTH CLUB TRAINER. ONE OF THEIR DAUGHTERS, ERIN, IS MARRIED TO A FIREFIGHTER, HAS TWO SONS, AND LIVES A FEW MILES NORTH OF THEM. THE TERBUSHES HAD THEIR HOME FOR THIRTY YEARS.

Larry: I'd gotten up and smelled smoke. I looked out the bedroom window toward the north and saw a little bit of glow in that direction. So I called Erin. Then I looked out our bathroom window to the east, where the fire came down the creek, and it was definitely glowing. I could see the bright bright red. I woke up Mary, and we started getting our things together.

Mary: We figured we'd be back. What I find so interesting is the things you grab. I grabbed some of my mother's jewelry that was irreplaceable emotionally. But I didn't bring any clothes. Larry got a folder of important papers and the computer.

Larry: I went into the garage, got a suitcase, and threw in our binders of photos—

Mary: I grabbed those. You grabbed water.

Larry (laughing): I grabbed a flat of bottled water that was on the shelf. I had no idea what the situation was going to be. The water was right there, we had space in the car, so I threw it in.

Mary: I had tunnel vision. I never thought of anything else except let's get the stuff and just go. I don't remember being nervous or scared. I just thought: Action!

Larry: We weren't doing a lot of talking, just methodically getting things together. We're very much alike, Mary and I, and I was very pleased with how we went through the whole thing that night.

Mary: We got to Erin's and just sat. Our grandsons Jake and Trent were wide awake. Erin had completely outfitted a bedroom for us. She got the bed ready and filled the drawers with pajamas and clothes and toiletries. Nobody went to sleep, we all just sat up and waited. I started getting a lot of phone calls about 7 A.M. from my brothers calling to check on me. Lots of phone calls from cousins. A friend in Australia.

Mary: When you said, "It's all gone," I was numb. How can you picture your house being gone? But when you said, "The whole neighborhood is gone," that hurt my heart. I felt that in my chest.

Mary: We were in constant contact with the kids in Ireland, back and forth phone calls. It was hard for them. They wanted to be here so badly, and they couldn't. As long as we talked to them every single day and kept them in the loop . . .

The fire was big news in Ireland, and the kids have many friends who approached them and asked, "Were your parents affected?" People there who knew us said, "We're so sorry to hear about your folks." I felt better knowing they were taken care of by friends.

It's still hard. They definitely realize they are so far away from what happened that they don't know exactly what it feels like. They see the photos, but it's so different to actually stand there in front of your destroyed home.

Larry: The squad I worked on did domestic and international terrorism, which in the seventies in San Francisco included a lot of bombings. Our squad worked all those crime scenes.

We had a saying after a bombing: "Everything is still here, it just changed shape." Of course, a fire consumes so much stuff. Most bombs don't burn, they just blow things apart.

Mary: You were not daunted when you looked at our pile of a house. I looked at it and said, "There's nothing here," but you looked right at it and focused.

Larry: Everything was still there. It just changed shape.

Mary: I don't wake up in the middle of the night anymore because I talk to a guy. Not a psychologist, a life coach. I went to him because I was worried I was handling it too well. I actually had two very well-meaning people come up to me and say, "I think that you're not grieving properly." I said, "OK, what do you want me to do?" I thought maybe I was missing something. I was waking up and having a hard time getting back to sleep, replaying that night like a movie.

After chatting with him, he said we could redirect my thinking. We really got into what makes me happy, what I'm grateful for. The hardest part was for me to feel worthy. More accepting of people's help. To me, there was always somebody who had it harder. But why wouldn't I feel worthy? I just lost my house!

Larry: I wish I'd found my dad's wedding ring, and his town marshal badge. Other than that . . . I still haven't gotten around to having my credentials and service medals replaced. They will be, but for some reason it really isn't a priority.

Mary: I miss the feeling of physically being in my mom's sitting room. That's gone. That room was a hub. It's not so much my things I'll miss, it's that I will no longer have that room. The week before the fire, Larry and I had our morning coffee in there and said, "This is the house we're going to live in the rest of our lives." ∎

KAREN AND I MET LARRY FOR LUNCH.

I'M SADDEST ABOUT LOSING OUR **HOME MOVIES**—FILM OF MY FATHER-IN-LAW PLAYING THE PIANO, OUR KIDS GROWING UP . . .

YEAH.

WE HAD VIDEOTAPES OF OUR GIRLS THAT I NEVER GOT AROUND TO DIGITIZING . . .

OH NO.

DAYS AND NIGHTS ARE LACED WITH TAUT EMOTIONAL TRIPWIRES WE BLUNDER THROUGH, AND THEN ARE SURPRISED EVERY TIME THEY EXPLODE.

A DAY IN THE NEW LIFE

THIRTEEN DAYS AFTER THE FIRE, THE ONLINE GRAPEVINE CAUGHT A RUMOR: TODAY THEY'D LET IN ONE CAR PER FAMILY. OUR GIRLS JOINED US AT THE NEAREST BARRICADE.

WE WERE TOLD THAT RESIDENTS COULD RE-ENTER?

CHECK WITH THE DEPUTIES DOWN AT THE NEXT INTERSECTION.

I'M NOT SURE WHEN YOU CAN GO IN. MAYBE THIS AFTERNOON?

ASK THE OFFICER ON YOUR STREET.

BUT HE SAID TO COME HERE . . .

I'M SORRY, BUT I JUST ARRIVED FROM SACRAMENTO. I DON'T EVEN KNOW THE NAME OF THIS STREET WE'RE ON!

WE FOUND A LINE SPONTANEOUSLY FORMING ON A MAIN ROAD AND JOINED IT, NOT AT ALL SURE WHAT IT WAS FOR.

THE KIT WAS A LARGE PLASTIC TRASH BAG THAT HELD:

ONE PAIR OF TYVEK
COVERALLS AND SHOE
COVERS PER PERSON

ONE DUST MASK PER
PERSON

ONE PAIR OF LATEX
GLOVES PER PERSON

ONE BOTTLE OF WATER
PER PERSON

ONE BOOK ON DISASTER
RECOVERY WE'D ALREADY
BEEN GIVEN SEVERAL
COPIES OF

THREE PAGES OF
INSTRUCTIONS ON
HANDLING HAZARDOUS
WASTE

IT TOOK US A FEW SECONDS TO FIGURE IT OUT: THE FIRE HAD HAPPENED ON GARBAGE DAY. THE BLACK BLOTCHES IN FRONT OF EVERY HOUSE WERE LIQUIDATED **TRASH CANS**.

STILL, OUR HOMES WERE HAZARDOUS WASTE SITES. THE FIRE BURNED NOT JUST WOOD AND PAPER, BUT PLASTIC, INSULATION, FIBERGLASS, AND ALL TYPES OF POTENTIAL POISONS. OUR ASHES WERE A CHEMICAL STEW.

DON'T FORGET YOUR DUST MASKS!

AND BE SURE TO TAKE OFF AND BAG EVERYTHING BEFORE YOU GET BACK INTO THE CAR!

OUR FIRST FIND: HOLIDAY DECORATIONS THAT HAD BEEN STORED IN THE GARAGE RAFTERS.

HERE'S CHRISTMAS.

THESE LOOK LIKE HALLOWEEN.

A LOT WAS RECOGNIZABLE BUT **UNSALVAGEABLE:** BLACK, BRITTLE, BROKEN.

WE PUT ANYTHING WE COULD IDENTIFY ON A TARP IN THE DRIVEWAY FOR SORTING.
NOT ALL OF IT WAS WORTH KEEPING, BUT IT ALL DESERVED AT LEAST A LAST LOOK.

Autumn decor

2007 Harvey Award, Best New Talent

Baking ramekins in perfect condition

Silver Christmas candle holder

Easter bunnies

Coin bank none of us remembers

Toy tea set

Thanksgiving cornucopia

Kids' bedroom door nameplates

Ladle my dad cooked with at summer logging camp as an Oregon teenager

MY SECOND GRAPHIC NOVEL WAS TITLED *WHATEVER HAPPENED TO THE WORLD OF TOMORROW?* WE WENT TO QUITE A BIT OF EFFORT TO PRINT IT ON **TWO** TYPES OF PAPER:

GLOSSY WHITE FOR MOST OF THE BOOK, AND A YELLOWER PULP PAPER FOR INSERTS THAT WERE MEANT TO LOOK LIKE OLD COMIC-BOOK PAGES.

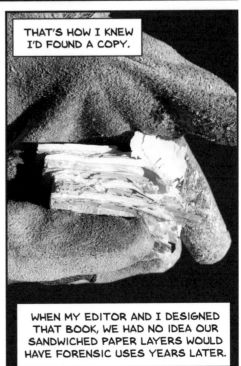

THAT'S HOW I KNEW I'D FOUND A COPY.

WHEN MY EDITOR AND I DESIGNED THAT BOOK, WE HAD NO IDEA OUR SANDWICHED PAPER LAYERS WOULD HAVE FORENSIC USES YEARS LATER.

AMONG THE ITEMS RECOVERED: TWO STEEL CANS FILLED WITH PENNIES EMPTIED FROM PANTS POCKETS OVER THE DECADES, THE CANS AND COINS FUSED INTO CYLINDERS OF SOLID SLAG.

I LEFT THEM ON THE TARP AND DIDN'T GIVE THEM ANOTHER THOUGHT.

DAYS LATER, A FIRE CREW WAS LAYING WATTLES TO CONTROL RAIN RUNOFF AND EROSION.

GOOD MORNING! IS THIS YOUR PROPERTY, SIR?

IT'S ALL MINE!

I NOTICED THOSE CONTAINERS OF COINS IN YOUR DRIVEWAY.

THESE MEN FROM THE DEPARTMENT OF CORRECTIONS NOTICED THEM, TOO.

I MADE SURE THEY ALL STAYED CLEAR . . .

I REALLY APPRECIATE THAT, BUT IF ANYONE WANTS FIVE BUCKS' WORTH OF MELTED CHANGE, THEY'RE WELCOME TO IT!

A DAY IN THE NEW LIFE

JERRY'S FIRE STORY

JERRY DUNN RECENTLY RETIRED FROM A FORTY-THREE-YEAR CAREER IN SOCIAL SERVICES. HE CARED FOR HIS PARTNER, BILL, WHO AT THE TIME OF THE FIRE WAS SEVENTY AND HAD ALZHEIMER'S DISEASE. THEIR HOUSEMATE, REYNOLDS, WAS NINETY-ONE. THEY LIVED IN SANTA ROSA'S FOUNTAINGROVE NEIGHBORHOOD.

What woke me up was the power outage. I sleep with—or *used to* sleep with, I haven't since the fire—a CPAP mask because I have sleep apnea. So when the power went out the CPAP stopped, and that woke me up.

It was 12:30 in the morning, I remember that vividly. The wind was howling, and the branches of the trees were pounding on our house. I could see out our bedroom window to the east, and all I saw was black. The key thing is, I didn't see any fire.

But I was creeped out. I did training one time about personal safety awareness, and one of the things they said was, if your instincts tell you something's wrong, trust your instincts. I wish I had taken that advice that night, because I felt like something was wrong and I talked myself out of it. I told myself, "Why are you spooked by the wind?"

It was about 2:15 when I heard a lot of cars going down our street. So I got up and walked into the living room, where my windows had a 180-degree view. There I saw the fire coming from a direction I couldn't see before. It looked close.

I yelled at the guys to get up. I had to help Bill get dressed. I put a T-shirt on him but didn't put his arms into it, so it was just hanging around his neck. We fixed that later in the car.

All of a sudden there was a pounding on our door. It was the Santa Rosa police, and they said, "You need to get out now. When you pull out of your driveway, turn left—that's the only way you can go."

We didn't have time to think about what to take. We got in the garage and Reynolds said to me, "How are you going to open the door without power?" I said, "Oh, just watch me!" I released the latch, and although it was a heavy sucker and I've struggled lifting it before, with adrenaline, it was no problem.

No matter how much reality is staring you in the face, denial is so powerful. We pulled out into the driveway, live red embers falling everywhere like rain, and I was starting to worry the car might catch on fire. But I stopped and got out. Reynolds said, "What the hell are you doing?" I said, "I'm gonna pull down the garage door! I don't want people to steal our stuff!" Because it never occurred to me I wouldn't be coming back, even in that extreme situation.

The thing I remember so vividly, I'll never forget this: We got on the freeway going south and I looked in my rearview mirror, and it looked like all of Santa Rosa was on fire.

JERRY LEARNED TWO DAYS LATER THAT HIS HOME WAS GONE WHEN A FRIEND OF HIS SON'S SHOT VIDEO OF THE SCENE.

It didn't feel real at first. Our family was intact, and that's what mattered. We were in a hotel. I knew I had to find more permanent shelter, and I knew that was going to be hard to do. We needed a staging area: someplace we wouldn't have to move out of every night, preferably something that wasn't a hotel where we'd have to go out to eat every meal. That was difficult on Bill.

I started to house-hunt. That was my project. That and getting a car for Reynolds, so if I was gone they weren't stranded. Like Maslow's hierarchy of needs, right? You need this first, then you need that next.

The most difficult thing about all this was turning old stuff off and getting new stuff on—the utility company, the phone company. I made thirty calls to AT&T, and each one lasted at least half an hour.

JERRY IS ALSO A SONGWRITER.

I lost more than a hundred pieces of songs I wrote but never finished. I had a cassette tape of about thirty songs I wrote and recorded on a cheap keyboard in the eighties, and I always wanted to go back and redo them. Now they're gone.

THE SAME DAY THEY MOVED INTO A LONG-TERM RENTAL, REYNOLDS FELL AND BROKE HIS HIP.

That was the icing on the cake. Poor Reynolds. He's a great patient, but he had a week when the doctors insisted his hip wasn't broken and he was miserable, in great pain. He could hardly walk at all. Reynolds really helps immensely with Bill. I was trying to do all this stuff, then trying to take care of both of them.

I'm a lousy nurse anyway. I remember I just sat down and thought, "I'm not going to be able to get through this." But Reynolds recovered and so did I.

BEFORE ALZHEIMER'S, BILL HAD BEEN A SUCCESSFUL INTERIOR DESIGNER.

Bill designed some of our furniture and set up a lot of our house. If he had his full faculties, he'd probably almost enjoy this. What fun to design the house all over again! He doesn't get to do that. The flip side is he doesn't seem to be overly concerned about it.

There are times, with all the work I'm doing to rebuild this house, that I ask, "Who am I doing it for?"

A couple of times Bill has said, "Well, we're going home today!" I tell him, "No, we're not, honey. We're not going home for a long time."

BILL'S ALZHEIMER'S DISEASE PROGRESSED QUICKLY FOLLOWING THE FIRE. THREE MONTHS AFTER THIS INTERVIEW WAS CONDUCTED, HE DIED. THREE WEEKS AFTER THAT, REYNOLDS DIED AFTER A BRIEF ILLNESS. THEY NEVER RETURNED HOME. ∎

A FEW DAYS AFTER OUR STREETS WERE OPENED TO RESIDENTS, THE BARRICADES CAME DOWN.

HEY, WHERE ARE THE COPS? WHERE'S THE NATIONAL GUARD?

I GUESS THEY FIGURED THEY GAVE US ENOUGH OF A HEAD START AND AREN'T NEEDED ANYMORE.

BUT WHAT ABOUT LOOTERS?! WE'RE DEFENSELESS!

FIRST YOU WERE MAD THEY WERE HERE. NOW YOU'RE MAD THEY'RE NOT!

A COUPLE OF WEEKS INTO OUR STAY AT THE GIRLS' PLACE, WE HAD TO PUT DOWN OUR CAT, AMBER.

SHE'D BEEN DECLINING FOR A WHILE. HER VET DREW BLOOD FOR LAB TESTS THE DAY BEFORE THE FIRE BUT THEN HAD TO CLOSE FOR A WEEK AFTERWARD, LEAVING US IN THE DARK.

AS SICK AS AMBER WAS, THE STRESS OF EVACUATING AND MOVING TO AN UNFAMILIAR PLACE CERTAINLY DIDN'T HELP.

WE ONLY GOT THE LAB RESULTS AFTER SHE WAS GONE. WE'D DONE THE RIGHT THING.

BUT IT WAS ONE MORE BOULDER TO ADD TO OUR ALREADY INCONCEIVABLY MASSIVE MOUNTAIN OF LOSS.

MIGUEL SAYS ALL THE RIGHT, REASSURING WORDS.

WE AGREED TO REBUILD YOUR HOME THE WAY IT WAS. THAT'S WHAT WE'RE GONNA DO.

IT REMAINS TO BE SEEN WHAT HIS COMPANY WILL ACTUALLY DO.

THE PARADOX: IT'LL PROBABLY COST MORE TO REBUILD MY HOUSE THAN IT AND THE LAND IT'S ON WERE WORTH IN THE FIRST PLACE.

WE'RE UNDERINSURED. **EVERYBODY** IS. SOME TAKE ONE LOOK AT THE NUMBERS AND LEAVE FOR CHEAPER STATES.

HOW MANY PROPERTIES HAVE YOU SEEN?

OH, I COULDN'T GUESS. DOZENS!

I DREW THIS DIAGRAM OF OUR DECK . . .

THAT'S A BIG HELP!

I ASSUMED INSURANCE COMPANIES ALL FOLLOW SIMILAR STANDARD INDUSTRY PRACTICES. THEY DON'T. EVEN **WITHIN** A COMPANY, WHAT THEY PROVIDE AND DEMAND VARIES ENORMOUSLY.

LUCKILY, OUR INSURER DID **NOT** REQUIRE WHAT MANY OTHERS DID: A VALUATION OF EVERYTHING THEIR CLIENTS OWNED.

EVERY PLATE, CUP, FORK, POT, PAN, MICROWAVE, WAFFLE IRON, COOKBOOK, BOWL, COFFEE MAKER, MIXER, BLENDER, TOASTER, TUMBLER, DISH TOWEL, TEA CUP, TONG, AND TRIVET.

EVERY COUCH, CHAIR, FOOTSTOOL, END TABLE, COFFEE TABLE, BOOKCASE, BOOK, MIRROR, RUG, CARPET, CABINET, LAMP, CURTAIN, PILLOW, CLOCK, TOWEL, BLANKET, BEDSHEET, TV, CD, AND DVD.

EVERY SHIRT, SKIRT, SWEATER, SUIT, DRESS, PANTS, SHORTS, SOCKS, SHOES, BOOTS, COAT, AND TIE; EVERY BICYCLE, LADDER, RAKE, SHOVEL, SCREWDRIVER, SPRINKLER, AND HOSE.

EVERY LAPTOP, TABLET, MONITOR, TELEPHONE, SCANNER, DESK, FILING CABINET, STORAGE CHEST, PAPER CLIP, STAPLER, NOTEPAD, CALENDAR, SCISSORS, THINGAMAJIG, KNICKKNACK, AND DOODAD.

EVERY THING.

WE'D LIKE TO SAVE THESE BIG LANDSCAPING ROCKS.

MM-HM.

FRIENDS SPENT **WEEKS** DOING INVENTORIES, COMBING THEIR MEMORIES ROOM BY ROOM, RELIVING LOSSES ONE AT A TIME.

HOW SENSELESS AND **SADISTIC.**

IF AN INSURANCE COMPANY AGREED TO COVER ALL YOUR POSSESSIONS FOR X DOLLARS, AND ALL YOUR POSSESSIONS WERE DESTROYED, SHOULDN'T THEY THEN PAY YOU X DOLLARS?

DO YOU THINK WE SHOULD TRY TO MOVE THE ROCKS OUT OF THE WAY?

HARD TO SAY . . .

EVIDENTLY NOT.

WE NAGGED MIGUEL ABOUT ROCKS FOR TEN MINUTES.

YOU KNOW, YOU CAN ALWAYS BUY MORE ROCKS.

THE ROCKS ARE ALL WE HAVE LEFT!

I BEGAN MY REPLY AS A **JOKE**, A PARODY OF A WILD OVERREACTION TO A TRIVIAL PROBLEM.

WHEN IT WAS HALFWAY OUT OF MY MOUTH, I REALIZED IT WAS **TRUE.**

I'M SORRY.

HERE'S MY CARD . . .

THE ROCKS WERE UNBURNABLE, IMMOBILE, ETERNAL— THE ONE THING THE FIRE COULDN'T TAKE AWAY FROM US.

THEY WERE LITERALLY **TOUCHSTONES** OF OUR LOST LIVES.

A DAY IN THE NEW LIFE

I READ AN ARTICLE BY A PSYCHOLOGIST WHO SAID PEOPLE LIKE US NEEDED TO FEEL **NORMAL** AGAIN, SO WE SHOULD DO ORDINARY THINGS WE USED TO ENJOY.

ONE OF MY FAVORITE SMALL INDULGENCES WAS BUYING A SANDWICH AND A DRINK, AND PICNICKING IN A SMALL TOWN GREEN A FEW MILES AWAY.

THAT SOUNDED WORTH A SHOT.

BLUE SKY, GREEN GRASS, SUNSHINE.

TEENAGERS HOLDING HANDS. HAPPY PEOPLE WALKING DOGS AND PUSHING BABY STROLLERS.

IT WAS **AWFUL**.

SLURRRP!

HALFWAY THROUGH MY LUNCH I REALIZED I DIDN'T **WANT** TO FEEL NORMAL. I COULDN'T EVEN IMAGINE WHAT "NORMAL" WOULD FEEL LIKE. WHAT I **REALLY** WANTED WAS FOR EVERYONE ELSE TO BE **MISERABLE**.

WATCHING THEM LIVE THEIR UNMISERABLE LIVES WAS **INFURIATING**. I ATE FAST AND LEFT.

THE ONLY TWO HOMES I'VE BOUGHT WERE ALREADY BUILT WHEN I GOT THEM. NOW WE DIDN'T KNOW WHERE TO BEGIN.

MY DREAM SOLUTION: AN EXPERIENCED DEVELOPER WHO'D SWOOP IN AND SAY:

WE HAVE SIX PLANS. PICK ONE AND WE'LL BUILD IT FOR YOU!

WHY NOT? HERE WERE THOUSANDS OF EAGER CUSTOMERS WILLING TO PAY SOMEONE TO SOLVE THEIR PROBLEMS! THERE WAS A **FORTUNE** TO BE MADE!

BUT THE BUSINESS DOESN'T WORK LIKE THAT. DEVELOPERS BUILD SUBDIVISIONS ON LAND OWNED BY **ONE** PARTY, OFTEN THEMSELVES, NOT HUNDREDS OF INDIVIDUAL LANDOWNERS WHO ALL HAVE UNIQUE FINANCES AND NEEDS.

ONE CONTRACT, NOT HUNDREDS.

OUR LIST OF SUITORS WAS SHORT.

103

ANOTHER DEVELOPER INTRODUCED THEMSELVES WITH A VIDEO TOUTING THEIR FAMILY VALUES AND COMMUNITY INVOLVEMENT. THEY LOOKED PRETTY GOOD UNTIL THE DEAD MOOSE.

... AS HUSBAND AND WIFE, THEY EMBARKED ON NEW ADVENTURES ...

I KNOW WILDLIFE HAS TO BE MANAGED, AND HUNTING SUPPORTS LOCAL ECONOMIES AND CONSERVATION. IT JUST SEEMED A STRANGE THING TO BRAG ABOUT IN A JOB INTERVIEW.

... SUPPORTED THE DIVERSIFICATION OF HOME OWNERSHIP ...

THAT WAS THE MOMENT I DECIDED I WASN'T PAYING FOR THESE RICH TWITS' NEXT BULLWINKLE SAFARI.

... PURSUED THEIR SHARED PASSION FOR HOMEBUILDING ...

WEEKS LATER, THEY PULLED OUT BECAUSE MATERIAL AND LABOR COSTS WERE TOO VOLATILE FOR THEM TO HIT THEIR PROMISED PRICES, LEAVING MANY EX-CLIENTS FLOUNDERING.

... AND GAVE BACK TO THE COMMUNITIES THEY SERVE ...

AFTER LIVING WITH OUR GIRLS A MONTH, WE FOUND A RENTAL THROUGH AN IN-LAW OF A WOMAN KAREN WORKS WITH. EVERY GOOD BREAK COMES VIA FRIENDS AND LUCK.

WE FOUND OUR HOMEBUILDER STANDING ON THE CORNER TALKING TO OUR NEIGHBOR, WHO'S BEEN HIS DEAR FRIEND FOR DECADES. HER OPINION MEANS A LOT, AND WE LIKE THAT HE'S LOCAL.

OUR DAUGHTER ROBIN IS AN ARCHAEOLOGIST WHO KNOWS HOW TO DIG UP ARTIFACTS.

OUR OTHER DAUGHTER, LAURA, IS A MUSEUM PROFESSIONAL WHO KNOWS HOW TO PRESERVE AND RESTORE THEM.

THE HUSBAND OF KAREN'S FORMER BOSS IS A RETIRED ARCHITECT.

A FRIEND OF MANY YEARS IS A SOILS ENGINEER.

A COLLEAGUE OF KAREN'S IS OUR COUNTY'S HEAD OF BUILDING PERMITS.

THE HUSBAND OF THE SISTER OF A CLOSE FRIEND FROM HIGH SCHOOL IS A RETIRED GENERAL CONTRACTOR.

NOT **ONCE** IN MY LIFE HAD I NEEDED TO BUILD A HOME, DIG UP ARTIFACTS, PRESERVE AND RESTORE THEM, DRAFT A BLUEPRINT, ENGINEER SOILS, PULL A BUILDING PERMIT, OR EVEN HIRE A GENERAL CONTRACTOR. NOW I HAD TO DO THEM **ALL**. THE LEARNING CURVE WAS A CLIFF. EVERYONE WAS GENEROUS WITH THEIR ADVICE. TO WEATHER THIS DISASTER, WE'D HAVE TO WORK EVERY ANGLE AND CALL IN EVERY FAVOR WE COULD.

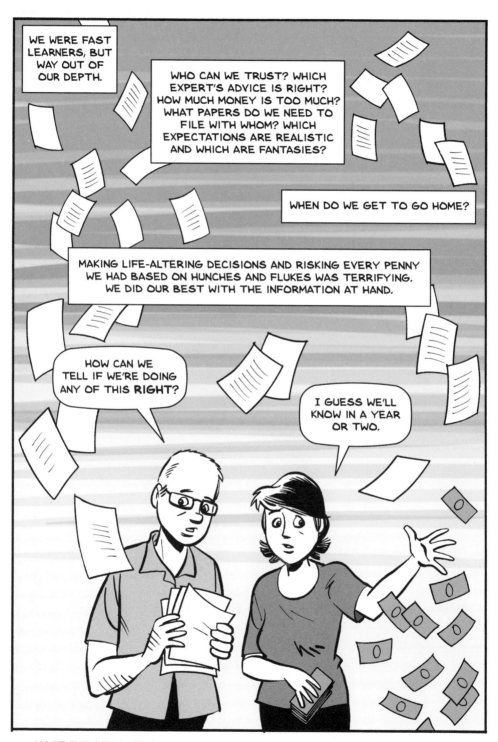

MORE THAN I'D LIKE, OUR FATE DEPENDED ON THE KINDNESS OF STRANGERS.

OUR RENTAL HOUSE WAS IN A SEMI-RURAL AREA. IT WASN'T UNUSUAL TO SMELL FIREPLACE SMOKE.

THIS WAS DIFFERENT.

HEY, I'M GONNA TAKE A LITTLE DRIVE AND SEE WHERE THAT SMOKE'S COMING FROM!

OUT IN THE COUNTRY, IT'S LEGAL TO BURN YARD WASTE: LEAVES, GRASS, BRANCHES.

EVERYTHING'S FINE.

I DIDN'T THINK MUCH OF IT UNTIL A FEW DAYS LATER, WHEN I MENTIONED IT TO A MAN WHO ALSO LOST HIS HOUSE IN THE FIRE, AND HE CONFESSED HE'D CHASED DOWN A HARMLESS SMOKE PLUME, TOO.

I WOULDN'T HAVE BEEN SO ALERT AND DILIGENT **BEFORE** MY HOME BURNED DOWN.

I SEE IT AS A SOCIALLY RESPONSIBLE FORM OF **PTSD.**

A DAY IN THE NEW LIFE

WE'RE GOING TO HAVE A HARD TIME SENDING CHRISTMAS CARDS WITHOUT OUR ADDRESS BOOK.

I'VE GOT IT!

WE KEPT THE ENVELOPES WITH THE CARDS WE RECEIVED **LAST** YEAR!

WE CAN JUST USE THEIR RETURN ADDRESSES!

GIVE IT A MINUTE . . .

WHAT?

OH.

RIGHT.

THE FIRE HIT WEEKS BEFORE OUR FAMILY'S FAVORITE
HOLIDAYS: HALLOWEEN, THANKSGIVING, CHRISTMAS.

MANY OF OUR BEST TRADITIONS—
DECORATIONS, RECIPES, COOKWARE,
DINNERWARE, GAMES, MOVIES,
MUSIC—WERE GONE. WE'D HAVE
TO COME UP WITH **NEW** ONES.

EVERY DECEMBER FOR MANY YEARS, KAREN AND I HAVE GIVEN LAURA
AND ROBIN AN **ADVENT CALENDAR** WITH TWENTY-FOUR TINY BOXES,
EACH HOLDING A SMALL GIFT TO BE OPENED IN THE DAYS LEADING UP
TO CHRISTMAS. OF COURSE IT WAS DESTROYED IN THE FIRE.

AT THE START OF NOVEMBER—A MONTH EARLY—OUR GIRLS GAVE AN ADVENT CALENDAR TO US.

WHAT? HOW? THIS LOOKS JUST LIKE OURS!

WHERE ON EARTH DID YOU FIND IT?

EVERYTHING'S ON THE INTERNET!

NOT EVERY GIFT FIT INTO A TINY BOX. LARGER ONES WERE WRAPPED SEPARATELY AND NUMBERED.

WHERE'S NUMBER ONE?

GOT IT!

IT'S THE GRINCH!

YAY! YOU SAVED CHRISTMAS!

THE GIRLS GAVE US VIDEOS AND MUSIC ALBUMS. HAND-BEADED BRACELETS AND HOMEMADE APRONS.

THEY FOUND **IMPOSSIBILITIES**. OBSCURE DOLLS AND OUT-OF-PRINT BOOKS. EPHEMERA FROM THE 1939 WORLD'S FAIR. A COMPLETE SET OF HARDY BOYS MYSTERIES.

EACH DAY OF NOVEMBER, OUR DAUGHTERS DID ONE SMALL, THOUGHTFUL THING THAT HELPED MAKE US WHOLE.

FRIENDS AND EXTENDED FAMILY RALLIED, TOO.

A WOMAN I ONCE WORKED WITH FOUND COLLECTABLE ORNAMENTS WE'D HUNTED DOWN TOGETHER TWENTY-FIVE YEARS AGO.

ONE OF KAREN'S SISTERS HAD SAVED EVERY HOMEMADE CHRISTMAS CARD WE'D SENT HER FOR THIRTY YEARS, AND RETURNED THEM ALL.

MY SISTERS GAVE US A PLASTIC CANDLE HOLDER WE CRAFTED WITH MOM WHEN I WAS A BOY.

ON CHRISTMAS EVE, WE STOOD OUR REPLACEMENT PLASTIC LIGHT-UP SANTA ON THE PORCH OF OUR RENTAL, AND HUNG NEW KNIT STOCKINGS UNDER A SILVER FIBER-OPTIC TREE.

MY COMPUTER MONITOR ON THE DINING ROOM TABLE PLAYED AN INFINITE LOOP OF FIREPLACE LOGS ABLAZE.

IT WASN'T LIKE ANY CHRISTMAS WE'D EVER HAD BEFORE.

BUT IT WASN'T TERRIBLE, EITHER.

SOME NEIGHBORS WERE SO WOUNDED THEY NEVER HAD THE HEART TO RETURN AT ALL.

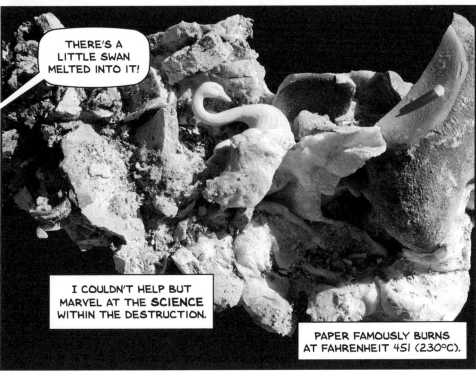

CONCRETE FOUNDATIONS POP, FLAKE, AND CRUMBLE AROUND 500°F (260°C).

AT ABOUT 1,200°F (650°C), THE ALUMINUM LEGS OF GRILLS MELT INTO RIVULETS THAT SEEP INTO THE EARTH.

GLASS LIGHT FIXTURES AND PATIO LAMPS LIQUEFY AT AROUND 1,400°F (760°C).

A THIRTEEN-INCH BRONZE TROPHY MELTS DOWN TO ITS BASE AT 1,500°F (790°C).

COPPER WATER PIPES TIE THEMSELVES INTO KNOTS NEAR 2,000°F (1,100°C).

MAJOR APPLIANCES AND MASSIVE STEEL I-BEAMS DOUBLE OVER AS IF PUNCHED IN THE GUT AROUND 2,600°F (1,400°C).

117

MY DAUGHTER LAURA SCRUBBED CONCRETE AND CERAMICS WITH A SODIUM CARBONATE SLURRY, FOLLOWED BY A SPRITZ OF HYDROGEN PEROXIDE.

THE MIXTURE OF BASE AND OXIDIZER HELPED FIZZ AWAY THE DIRT AND ASH.

ROBIN COULDN'T WAIT TO ATTACK OUR SITE.

SHE BORROWED A TRUNKFUL OF ARCHAEOLOGY GEAR FROM HER OFFICE AND ASSEMBLED A TEAM.

BY THE TIME THEY GOT TO OUR RUINS, WE'D ALREADY GONE OVER THEM PRETTY WELL. THEY DIDN'T DIG UP MUCH.

IN ONE WAY THAT WAS DISAPPOINTING. THERE WAS STILL SO MUCH WE'D HOPED TO FIND.

IN ANOTHER WAY IT WAS A RELIEF. IF THIS CREW COULDN'T FIND SOMETHING, IT PROBABLY WASN'T GOING TO BE FOUND. KNOWING WE'D DONE OUR BEST MADE IT EASIER TO LET GO.

Archaeology 101

A standard archaeological tool is the rocking screen, a wooden frame about two feet square with metal mesh and two hinged legs.

 1.

With the screen lying on the ground, fill it with one bucket of debris to be examined.

 2.

Grasp the screen and pull it up in one confident fluid motion.

3.

Skitter the screen's legs over the ground until the frame whacks your shins.

Curse.

4.

Bracing a hinged leg with your foot, grasp the screen and pull it up in one confident fluid motion.

5.

Shake the screen vigorously to sift small particles and dust. Apologize to anyone downwind.

6.

While supporting the screen with one hand, use a trowel to examine debris. Imagine you saw something shiny; fail to find it. Lose your place and start over.

7.

When done, tip debris onto waste pile. Apologize to anyone downwind.

Repeat.

AID GROUPS SENT AROUND CRISIS COUNSELORS FROM TIME TO TIME.

THEY WERE KIND, EARNEST PEOPLE WHO MEANT PAINFULLY WELL . . .

126

I AM UPROOTED.

SUNNY'S FIRE STORY

BRADLEY SUNSHINE HACKWELL AND HIS GIRLFRIEND, KATELYN, LIVED IN THE HILLS BETWEEN CALISTOGA AND SANTA ROSA, IN THE PATH OF THE TUBBS FIRE. SUNNY, TWENTY-SIX, IS A CONSTRUCTION WORKER WHO SERVED WITH THE U.S. ARMY IN AFGHANISTAN.

I was working security for an Indian casino at the time. I worked really early in the morning, so I was already in bed by 9 P.M. Around 11:30 my girlfriend and our roommate woke me up saying, "Get up, we've gotta get out of the house!" I was pissed because I had to wake up early and thought my friend was playing a joke on me. When I saw Katelyn's face, I knew something was wrong.

I went outside immediately and could see a glow above the tree line. I thought, "Holy crap, this is real!" My roommate's already gone, he's down the road. As I ran back inside to grab Katelyn, the power turned off, so I knew the fire was close.

We hopped into her Tahoe and as soon as we turned onto the main road, everything was engulfed in flames. Left side and right side. With the wind, it looked like waves of flame rolling across the road. Our windows were up but you could feel the heat inside the vehicle, like a sunburn on your face.

Katelyn's freaking out. I've been in worse situations, so I'm quiet. I'm just trying to get through it and calm her down. It's a bad situation, you've got to keep your cool, but if you stop moving, your tires melt and you die.

What I took out of the Army and used in the fire is this: you can't freak out. You've got to stay stress-free and focus on what you're doing. Take emotion out of it. If you freeze, if you take a breath, you could lose your chance at either breathing again or saving a friend.

In Afghanistan, there were a lot of situations where I didn't know what to do. I just knew what was in front of me and what I *could* do at that moment.

A couple of cars slowed down because there were flames in front of us, so I swerved in front of them and gunned it. They fell in right behind me, and before I know it there's two, three, four cars behind us and I'm leading the way through a firestorm.

I did two tours, four years—10th Mountain Division, 1st Battalion, 32nd Infantry Regiment. South Kandahar Province. We basically patrolled, and for six months we built COPs (command operating posts) for the Afghan National Army. It's called "peacekeeping"—kind of like being a police officer, you just walk around and have a presence to deter stupid things from happening. Which, really honestly, just set us up for getting shot at.

How you respond in a situation has more to do with experience than training. Just because someone teaches you something doesn't mean you're going to do it right.

I was building a tower during my first deployment in Afghanistan. We had to stack sandbags. And we hear two pops and two snaps. A pop shot is when you hear gunfire. The snap? That's a bullet breaking the sound barrier, which means it's next to you. So if you hear a pop shot, you just keep walking normal. But if you hear a snap, you get down. Real quick. Or you return fire.

I'd probably been shot at seven or eight times in the first month I was there, so I was used to it, but not like I was at the end of my deployment, when I was keen to every sound and sight. So we're getting the sandbags stacked all nice, and we hear two snaps go by. And then two more snaps. Then the wood cracks right next to us on the top of the tower.

One guy jumps off the tower, another rolls into the tower, and I'm standing there with a sandbag in my hands. Just standing there, not moving. My buddy says, "Get down, you idiot!" and grabs my boot and pulls me inside the tower.

I didn't have experience then. I got a lot more practice after that.

We made it through the firestorm to a bunch of sheriff's cars. The fire's maybe twenty or thirty feet behind us. They rushed us through and we all met at a parking lot to make sure everybody got out and was fine.

After that, Katelyn and I went to the casino hotel and watched the news to see if our house burned down. Sure enough, it did. Me being a casino employee, I had a hook on a room, so we stayed there for three months and a week.

FEMA was no help. We'd been renting the bottom floor of a big three-story house. Other people lived on the other floors. So when I applied for FEMA, they had about nine or ten people applying from the same address. One person got approved and everybody else got denied. They couldn't understand how more than one household could live at one address. They thought it was a scam.

I burned through savings. I burned through everything just trying to survive. We didn't even know if we were going to be able to eat. Thank God I had family here or we would've been on the streets.

SUNNY'S LANDLORD, MIKE, WHOSE HOUSE ALSO BURNED DOWN, OFFERED HIM A CONSTRUCTION JOB.

Katelyn and I were going to move to Tennessee. California is just too expensive. But Mike gave me a job and kept me working. Now I'm making really good money.

It means a lot to help people rebuild their homes. I'm all about the community. I feel like I have to give more because I see everybody else giving more. There's always someone in worse shape than me. I'm blessed. ∎

A DAY IN THE NEW LIFE

CUTE SWEATER!

THANKS, IT'S NEW!

snerk!

"IT'S NEW!"

HEY, IT'S **ALL** NEW!

FROM TIME TO TIME, WE WALK OUR DOG, RILEY, THROUGH OUR OLD NEIGHBORHOOD.

SHE ACTS HAPPY AND EXCITED.

snf snf snf

SHE SEEMS TO KNOW THAT THIS IS HOME.

I THOUGHT I WAS DOING IT FOR **HER,** BUT SOON REALIZED I WAS REALLY DOING IT FOR **ME.**

WALKING MY DOG IS HOW I MARK **MY** TERRITORY. IT'S HOW I SAY, "THIS IS STILL MY TURF. I BELONG HERE."

BEING PART OF SOMETHING SO BIG MAKES **PERSPECTIVE** ELUSIVE.

DURING THE FIRE, WE LIVED IN A BUBBLE. WE SAW VERY LITTLE TELEVISION, HEARD NOTHING FROM THE WORLD OUTSIDE. FRIENDS AND RELATIVES ACROSS THE COUNTRY KNEW MORE ABOUT WHAT WAS HAPPENING HERE THAN WE DID.

WEEKS LATER, WE **STILL** LIVED IN A BUBBLE—A TINY BUBBLE OF **OUR** FAMILY, **OUR** PROPERTY, **OUR** LOSSES, **OUR** PROBLEMS.

THEN WE'D TAKE A DRIVE. MILE AFTER MILE, HOUR AFTER HOUR, RUIN AFTER RUIN: THOUSANDS OF OTHER PEOPLE'S BUBBLES AS REAL AND URGENT AS OURS.

THERE'S A RIDGE IN THE FOUNTAINGROVE NEIGHBORHOOD WHERE YOU CAN LOOK DOWN INTO A VALLEY A COUPLE OF MILES BELOW. ON THE OTHER SIDE OF THE VALLEY IS A DISTANT RIDGE THAT PARALLELS THE ONE YOU'RE ON. BEYOND THAT RIDGE, A FARTHER ROW OF HIGHER HILLS.

VIRTUALLY EVERYTHING YOU CAN SEE, FROM HORIZON TO HORIZON, BURNED THAT NIGHT.

ALL IN ALL, THE FIRE-STORMS CLAIMED ABOUT 350 SQUARE MILES (910 SQUARE KILOMETERS). IT'S A BIG NUMBER THAT BY ITSELF MEANS **NOTHING.**

IT'S ABOUT FIFTEEN MANHATTANS. SEVEN-AND-A-HALF SAN FRANCISCOS. ONE-AND-A-HALF CHICAGOS. ONE-THIRD OF RHODE ISLAND.

PERSPECTIVE: IT'S THE COMFORT AND HORROR OF REALIZING YOU'RE NOT ALONE.

WITHIN A FEW WEEKS OF THE FIRE, GREEN REAPPEARED AMID THE BLACK AND GRAY.

KAREN GREW NAKED LADIES—AMARYLLIS BELLADONNA—IN THE SHADE OF A BACKYARD TREE. I DUG THEM UP AS GENTLY AS I COULD AND TRANSPLANTED THEM TO A POT, WHERE THEY THRIVED. SOMEDAY THEY'D RETURN TO THIS SOIL, BUT UNTIL THEN THEY WERE COMING WITH US.

REDWOODS PUSHED OUT STUBBY SHOOTS BETWEEN DEAD, BURNED BRANCHES.

WEEKS LATER, ROSES POKED UP AS WELL. WE DON'T KNOW WHICH VARIETY—KAREN HAD SEVERAL—AND THEY MAY BE UNRECOGNIZABLE ANYWAY, SINCE ROSES ARE GROWN BY GRAFTING AND THE SURVIVING PLANTS ARE LIKELY THE UNRELATED ROOTSTOCKS.

SLEEPING BULBS STIRRED FROM THE EARTH. DAFFODILS WERE COMING.

WE'LL TRANSPLANT THEM, TOO, AND SEE WHAT BLOOMS.

AS A LITERARY METAPHOR, ALL THIS NEW GROWTH IS A CLICHÉ: "LIFE GOES ON." STILL, THAT DOESN'T MAKE IT UNTRUE, AND IT'S MARVELOUS TO SEE. FLOWERS AND TREES CAN COME BACK, CHANGED AND SCARRED BUT STILL BEAUTIFUL. SO CAN WE.

YOU GUYS RAISED A FAMILY HERE?

TWIN GIRLS, ALL GROWN UP.

I HAVE A BOY AND TWO GIRLS.

THEY GREW UP WITH SPANISH AND ENGLISH. THEN THEY LEARNED ITALIAN AND PORTUGUESE FROM OTHER FAMILIES WE LIVED WITH.

"LOOK FORWARD."

IT'S TOUGH TO DO WHEN EVERY DAY SEEMS LIKE A FRESH CRISIS. NOW WE HAVE NO CHOICE.

I'VE **LEARNED**, BUT IT'S HARD TO SAY WHAT. "APPRECIATE EVERY DAY TO ITS FULLEST," I GUESS.

THAT, AND, "IF YOU'RE EVER TOLD TO EVACUATE, ASSUME IT'S REAL AND YOU'LL NEVER SEE YOUR HOUSE AGAIN."

ALSO, "KNOW WHAT'S IN YOUR INSURANCE POLICY."

I'VE **CHANGED**, BUT IT'S HARD TO SAY HOW. MAYBE SOMETHING LIKE, "DON'T SWEAT THE SMALL STUFF."

PEOPLE SEEM TO WANT A STORY WITH UPLIFT AND CLOSURE, BUT I HAVE NO UPLIFT TO GIVE, AND ANYONE WHO SAYS "CLOSURE" AROUND ME MAY GET A PUNCH IN THE NOSE.

THERE'S NEVER CLOSURE. YOU JUST SLOWLY GET USED TO YOUR NEW LIFE.

IDEAS LIKE "FAMILY," "COMMUNITY," "TRADITION," AND "HOME" MEAN MORE TO ME NOW THAN THEY DID BEFORE.

HOME IS STILL THE PLACE YOU LIVE, THE STUFF INSIDE IT, AND THE PEOPLE WHO LIVE THERE AND BUILD MEMORIES WITH YOU.

TWO YEARS
LATER...

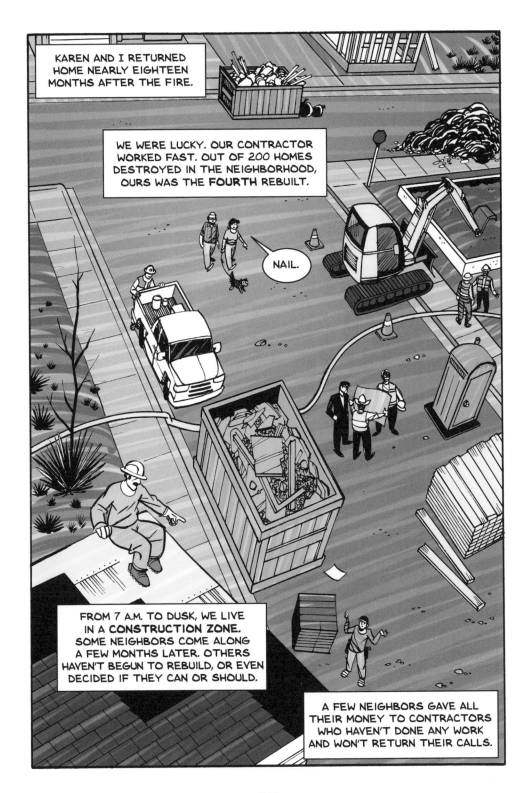

KAREN AND I RETURNED HOME NEARLY EIGHTEEN MONTHS AFTER THE FIRE.

WE WERE LUCKY. OUR CONTRACTOR WORKED FAST. OUT OF 200 HOMES DESTROYED IN THE NEIGHBORHOOD, OURS WAS THE **FOURTH** REBUILT.

NAIL.

FROM 7 A.M. TO DUSK, WE LIVE IN A **CONSTRUCTION ZONE**. SOME NEIGHBORS COME ALONG A FEW MONTHS LATER. OTHERS HAVEN'T BEGUN TO REBUILD, OR EVEN DECIDED IF THEY CAN OR SHOULD.

A FEW NEIGHBORS GAVE ALL THEIR MONEY TO CONTRACTORS WHO HAVEN'T DONE ANY WORK AND WON'T RETURN THEIR CALLS.

PEOPLE ASK IF WE MIND THE NOISE. WE ALWAYS SAY, "NO. THAT'S THE SOUND OF FRIENDS COMING HOME."

THAT WOULD'VE GONE RIGHT INTO A CAR TIRE!

THAT'S PARTLY TRUE.

BUT WE CANNOT WAIT FOR ALL OF THIS TO BE DONE.

A SAW BLADE?!

GOT IT.

WE CAN'T STEP OUTSIDE OUR DOOR WITHOUT DODGING TRASH, TRENCHES, TOILETS, AND GIANT TONKA TOYS.

WIND-BLOWN DUST AND GRIT ARE EVERYWHERE, INDOORS AND OUT.

WATCH THAT BROKEN GLASS!

MAYBE WE SHOULD BRING A BROOM ON OUR NEXT WALK.

THESE ARE PROBLEMS A LOT OF FOLKS WISH THEY HAD. WE'RE GRATEFUL TO THE HARD-WORKING BUILDERS, SOME FROM VERY DISTANT PLACES, WHO FOUND OPPORTUNITY IN OUR RECOVERY.

NOW WE'RE ITCHING TO BE LEFT ALONE.

A FEW CHARCOAL TREES STILL STAND ON NEGLECTED OR ABANDONED LOTS. OTHER TREES WILL NEED ANOTHER SEASON TO REVEAL WHETHER THEY'LL LIVE OR DIE.

TEMPORARY MAILBOXE

PUBLIC WORKS HASN'T REPLACED OUR MELTED STREETLIGHTS. WILDLIFE WANDERS THROUGH UNFENCED LOTS. IT'S VERY DARK AND QUIET AT NIGHT.

YAP
YAP YAP
YAPYAPYAP
YAP!

OUR NEIGHBORHOOD IS HALF WILD AND HALF TAMED, HALF ALIVE AND HALF DEAD, STITCHED TOGETHER WITH CONCRETE, PIPES, AND WIRE.

HOW MUCH LONGER?

THEY SAY WE'LL BE IN NEXT MONTH!

WE FOCUSED SO LONG AND HARD ON REBUILDING THAT WE ONLY REALIZED AFTER MOVING IN THAT IT DIDN'T MAGICALLY FIX EVERYTHING . . .

HEY, THAT'S GREAT.

IT'S SO EXCITING!

I'VE MET OTHER FIRE SURVIVORS WHO SHARE MY IRRATIONAL **SHAME** THAT I LET DOWN HISTORY.

I WAS THE KEEPER OF MY FAMILY'S PAST.

I HAD EVERYONE'S ANTIQUES FROM THE OLD COUNTRY. ALL THEIR **TREASURES.**

SOME OF THEM WERE MORE THAN 400 YEARS OLD!

MY GREAT-GRANDPARENTS PACKED THEM UP, BROUGHT THEM TO AMERICA, CARRIED THEM ACROSS THE COUNTRY, AND ENTRUSTED THEM TO ME.

AND I LET THEM BURN.

YOU KNOW THERE'S NOTHING YOU COULD HAVE DONE.

DOESN'T MATTER. IT HAPPENED ON MY WATCH.

IN THE CHAIN OF POSTERITY, WE WERE THE LINKS THAT BROKE.

RIGHT AFTER THE FIRE, OUR INSURANCE ADJUSTOR PROMISED US THEY'D REPLACE OUR HOUSE. THAT WASN'T ENTIRELY TRUE.

FIES.

FIES.

IN THE END, THEY PAID AS LITTLE AS POSSIBLE—IN OUR OPINION, LESS THAN THEY WERE OBLIGED TO—AND NOT A DIME MORE. SINCE WE WERE BADLY UNDERINSURED, WE NEEDED EVERY DIME WE COULD FIND.

F. I. E. S. NO, "S" AS IN "SAM."

INSURANCE COMPANIES AND THEIR APOLOGISTS SAY THE SAME THING: A POLICY IS A **CONTRACT** WHOSE TERMS WE AGREED TO AND SIGNED.

YES, I'LL HOLD.

UNDERSTANDING THOSE TERMS, AND MAKING SURE THE POLICY'S COVERAGE WAS ADEQUATE, WAS **OUR** RESPONSBILITY.

FINE.

BUT WHENEVER WE QUESTIONED THE AMOUNT OF OUR COVERAGE **BEFORE** THE FIRE, THE INSURANCE COMPANY ASSURED US THAT THEY KNEW THE LOCAL HOUSING AND CONSTRUCTION MARKETS, AND THEIR SOFTWARE WEIGHED MORE ECONOMIC VARIABLES THAN MERE HUMAN MINDS COULD COMPREHEND.

THEY WERE THE EXPERTS. WE WOULD HAVE HAPPILY PAID HIGHER PREMIUMS FOR MORE COVERAGE, BUT WE WERE NEVER GIVEN THAT OPTION.

BESIDES, WE TRUSTED THEM.

THAT WAS OUR MISTAKE.

EVEN **AFTER** THE FIRE, WHEN WE KNEW BETTER, GETTING PROPER COVERAGE WAS A STRUGGLE.

I'M CALLING TO SET UP HOMEOWNER'S INSURANCE FOR OUR NEW HOUSE.

BASED ON THE INFORMATION WE HAVE, WE'LL INSURE YOUR DWELLING FOR FOUR...

THAT'S ONLY A LITTLE MORE THAN YOU INSURED OUR **OLD HOUSE FOR!**

THAT'S WHAT THE COMPUTER SAYS IT WOULD COST TO REBUILD YOUR DWELLING.

WELL, I JUST REBUILT IT, SO I KNOW **EXACTLY** HOW MUCH IT WOULD COST ...

OH, GOOD!

... WHICH IS **TWICE** THAT MUCH!

♪ click.

MS. FIES?

I'M AUTHORIZED TO APPROVE 150 PERCENT OF THAT COVERAGE AMOUNT.

THAT'S NOT ENOUGH. I NEED ANOTHER 50 PERCENT.

THE COMPUTER WILL ONLY ALLOW ME TO GO UP TO 150 PERCENT.

SO WHO CAN I TALK TO TO BUY ENOUGH COVERAGE TO ACTUALLY REPLACE MY HOME?

UM . . . WE DON'T HAVE A PROCESS FOR THAT . . .

WE TOOK WHAT WE COULD GET AND LEFT THAT FIGHT FOR ANOTHER DAY. TRYING TO BE RESPONSIBLE ISN'T ALWAYS EASY OR ENOUGH.

153

THE MOST COMMON COMPLAINT ABOUT INSURANCE COMPANIES CONCERNS ADDITIONAL LIVING EXPENSES: **ALE**.

BY LAW, INSURERS HAVE TO PAY FOR **TWO YEARS** OF RENT WHILE THEIR CUSTOMERS' HOMES ARE REBUILT. THE PROBLEM: IT'S IMPOSSIBLE TO REPLACE THOUSANDS OF HOMES IN TWO YEARS.

A FEW INSURERS VOLUNTARILY EXTENDED **ALE** TO THREE YEARS. UNDER PRESSURE FROM THE CALIFORNIA DEPARTMENT OF INSURANCE, MORE EVENTUALLY DID THE SAME. BUT SOME OF THE BIGGEST COMPANIES STILL REFUSED, AND AS THE TWO-YEAR ANNIVERSARY PASSED, FIRE SURVIVORS WHO'D HOPED TO RETURN HOME WERE FORCED TO GIVE UP AND LEAVE THE AREA. WITHOUT **ALE**, THEY COULDN'T AFFORD TO STAY.

KAREN AND I WEREN'T AFFECTED—WE RETURNED HOME BEFORE THE DEADLINE—BUT JOINED THE PROTESTS JUST THE SAME.

NOT A GOOD NEIGHBOR

HOMELESS AGAIN!

PEOPLE OVER PROFIT!

YOU CAN'T REBUILD A CITY IN 24 MONTHS!

THE INSURERS' INDIFFERENCE WAS PART OF A BIGGER ISSUE. COMPANIES BASED IN TEXAS, OHIO, OR ILLINOIS WEREN'T **LOCAL**. THEY DIDN'T UNDERSTAND THE CHALLENGES OF RECOVERING FROM A HISTORIC WILDFIRE.

THE MORE FUNDAMENTAL PROBLEM: INSURANCE COMPANIES STAY PROFITABLE BY **KEEPING** AS MUCH MONEY AS THEY CAN, NOT BY PAYING IT BACK TO POLICYHOLDERS.

IN A CORNER OF OUR BACKYARD, WE HAD A LITTLE MOUND OF DIRT AND PLANTS. IN THE SHADOW OF A BIRDBATH WERE THE GRAVES OF OUR DOG AND TWO CATS.

AFTER THE FIRE, WE STAKED IT OFF AND ASKED EVERYONE NOT TO DISTURB IT. NO ONE DID.

THROUGH A YEAR AND A HALF OF CONSTRUCTION, THE MOUND WAS THE ONLY PATCH OF EARTH THAT WASN'T DUG, SCRAPED, PLOWED, OR FILLED.

FLOWERS BLOOMED AND WILTED WITH THE SEASONS. WILD BLACK-BERRIES TOOK ROOT.

IT WAS AN OASIS IN A DESERT.

WHEN ALL ELSE WAS GONE, IT ALSO BECAME AN ESSENTIAL LANDMARK.

NINE MONTHS AFTER THE FIRE, OUR CONTRACTOR OUTLINED OUR FOUNDATION IN CHALK AND HAD AN EXCAVATOR READY TO DIG.

THIS'LL BE THE KITCHEN.

WITH WINDOWS HERE . . .

THE FOOTPRINT OF OUR NEW HOUSE WAS NEARLY THE SAME AS THE OLD ONE'S. WE'D ALREADY LIVED IN THIS SPACE.

LOOK AT WHERE THE MOUND IS.

IT'S TOO CLOSE!

THEY'RE DIGGING IN THE WRONG PLACE!

STOP!

SOMETHING DOESN'T LOOK RIGHT!

WE MEASURED ALL THE SETBACKS . . .

MEASURE THEM AGAIN.

SEE? TWENTY FEET FROM HERE TO THE CORNER OF THE GARAGE . . .

BUT THE WAY THE STREET CURVES, SHOULDN'T WE MEASURE FROM OVER THERE?

OK, THAT MOVES THE BUILDING OVER A FEW FEET . . .

AND OUR SIDE YARD SETBACK WAS DIFFERENT, TOO.

ARE YOU SURE?

LOOK AT THIS PHOTO OF OUR OLD HOUSE:

SIX FENCE BOARDS AT SIX INCHES EACH, PLUS A FIVE-FOOT GATE, EQUALS EIGHT FEET!

159

OUR HOUSE GOT REBUILT WHERE WE WANTED, WITHIN A FOOT OR SO OF WHERE IT WAS BEFORE.

NEARLY A YEAR LATER, AFTER WE MOVED BACK, WE CLEANED UP THE MOUND. WE HACKED OUT THE WEEDS AND BLACK-BERRIES, AND MARVELED AT HOW WELL THE CORNER HAD THRIVED ON ITS OWN.

THE OLD WROUGHT IRON WAS USELESS AS A GATE, BUT INVALUABLE AS **ART**. I BOLTED IT TO FENCE POSTS BEHIND THE MOUND, BRACKETING THE SOOT-STAINED BIRDBATH.

ON A BOUNDLESS AND BARE PLAIN, THE MOUND AND GATE WERE THE BENCHMARKS THAT GUIDED US HOME.

AFTER WE MOVED IN, KAREN'S COWORKERS WANTED TO HELP US LANDSCAPE. WE PROVIDED THE MATERIALS AND LUNCH. THEY ASSEMBLED THE **TEAM**.

ABOUT TWO DOZEN PEOPLE SHOWED UP, SOME FOR AN HOUR AND OTHERS FOR ALL DAY. THEY DUG HOLES, SHOVELED GRAVEL, SPREAD BARK.

THEY DID A LOT OF HARD WORK ON A HOT DAY.

IN THE AFTERNOON, JUST AS OUR ENERGY WAS FLAGGING, A CHURCH YOUTH GROUP APPEARED. NOBODY KNEW WHO THEY WERE. THEY'D SOMEHOW HEARD WHAT WE WERE DOING AND WANTED TO HELP.

THEY WERE A VERY WELCOME MINOR MIRACLE.

IT WAS AN OLD-FASHIONED **BARN RAISING!**

IN ONE DAY WE LANDSCAPED OUR ENTIRE FRONT YARD AND PART OF THE BACK—WORK THAT WOULD HAVE COST US TENS OF THOUSANDS OF DOLLARS.

KAREN AND I FELT HOPELESSLY GRATEFUL. HOW DO YOU THANK SOMEONE FOR THAT? HOW CAN YOU POSSIBLY REPAY THEM?

WE'LL TRY TO PAY IT FORWARD AND DO THE SAME FOR OUR FRIENDS AND NEIGHBORS WHEN THEIR TURNS COME.

KINTSUGI IS THE CENTURIES-OLD JAPANESE ART OF REPAIRING BROKEN CERAMICS WITH **GOLD.**

INSTEAD OF TRYING TO **HIDE** DAMAGE, KINTSUGI HIGHLIGHTS AND CELEBRATES IT AS PART OF THE OBJECT'S HISTORY.

I HAVE A DEEP APPRECIATION FOR KINTSUGI AS I WATCH MY NEIGHBORHOOD REBUILD.

SOME SURVIVORS WANT ALL EVIDENCE OF THE FIRE ERASED—PLOWED UNDER, PAVED OVER, PAINTED AWAY.

I UNDERSTAND BUT DISAGREE.

I **LIKE** MY WARPED AND RUSTED IRON GATE, AND THE SPOTS WHERE OUR BURNING TRASH CANS MELTED THE STREET. THESE OCCASIONAL SMALL REMINDERS DON'T BOTHER ME.

THEY TELL OUR STORY. THEY'RE THE SCARS WE EARNED. OUR KINTSUGI.

AS THE TWO-YEAR ANNIVERSARY NEARED, WE HAD TO DECIDE WHETHER TO JOIN A LAWSUIT AGAINST OUR UTILITY, **PG&E**.

YOU DON'T SUE A TORNADO OR A HURRICANE! DISASTERS HAPPEN!

NATURAL DISASTERS. THAT'S THE QUESTION: WAS IT NATURAL?

SURE, POWER LINES FELL, BUT IF IT HADN'T BEEN FOR THE WIND, OUR FIRE WOULDN'T HAVE GONE ANYWHERE!

I KNOW . . .

WE DON'T WANT TO BE AMBULANCE CHASERS!

BUT WE DON'T WANT TO BE **STUPID**, EITHER.

IF A JUDGE AND JURY DECIDE THAT PG&E DID SOMETHING WRONG AND OUR HOUSE BURNED DOWN AS A RESULT, WE DESERVE COMPENSATION.

YOU KNOW IT'LL BE A BIG HASSLE, AND TEN YEARS FROM NOW WE'LL GET A CHECK FOR FIFTY-THREE BUCKS.

YEAH. PROBABLY.

SOUS

SOUS

CHOP CHOP

I'LL ASK ANN AND JEREMY WHO THEY'RE USING.

AFTER MONTHS OF EQUIVOCATING, WE JOINED.

JAMES'S FIRE STORY

AT THE TIME OF THE 2017 FIRESTORM, JAMES GORE WAS VICE-CHAIR OF THE SONOMA COUNTY BOARD OF SUPERVISORS—THE GOVERNMENT BODY WITH JURISDICTION OVER MOST OF THE BURN ZONE, MUCH OF WHICH FELL IN HIS DISTRICT. GORE BECAME CHAIRMAN IN JANUARY 2018. HE AND HIS COLLEAGUES AND STAFF WERE IN CHARGE OF DISASTER RESPONSE BOTH DURING THE FIRE AND IN THE MONTHS THAT FOLLOWED.

The day before the fires, I was as sick as I'd been in recent memory. Strep throat real bad. I was loaded up on penicillin. That night around midnight, my wife, Elizabeth, came in and said, "Your phones are blowing up." I got a message from a friend: "James, we're driving out of our neighborhood. Everything's on fire. I think our house is gone."

From that moment the adrenaline surge was just like Popeye eating spinach, and I was able to put that adrenaline into service. First thing I did was set up command central in my house. I had a computer up, I had two cell phones, and I was calling my staff and every single community leader or constituent I knew in those communities.

I learned from previous floods and smaller fires that people want information. They need information. They can't sleep until they get information. I could pull everything together and say, "Here's your information."

Do people want politicians like me to give big speeches? No, they want to know what the hell is going on. Too often, people in my position fight to be informed and then they don't share it, or they share it through sterile, sanitized talking points. I figured it out on the fly. I just drove into burn zones and started to post videos online. The first one got 10,000 views, then 40,000. A Spanish one I did got 200,000 views.

Every morning I did a video with the battalion chief to show me the fire map, and he appreciated that because then he didn't have to take calls about it the rest of the day. He could tell everybody, "Watch my video with Gore." It was the first real example to me of social media being a conduit for real news instead of fake news.

The way I look at it, you have to take all that energy, that fire, and, like a blacksmith, create something with it. Hammer it into policies and training. You never want to look back and say, "We didn't do everything we could have," like we said after 2017.

We had an emergency procedure called the Local Hazard Mitigation Plan. It was a dusty document instead of a living, breathing thing. Everybody—the county, our citizens, our organizations, our Department of Emergency Management—was prepared for slow-moving floods and fires. We acted like we had two days to get ready. We were prepared for business as usual, as opposed to when it literally rains fire.

In 2017, we had a significant red flag (high wind) warning; no one paid attention. We did not upstaff our fire departments for the red flag warning. We had not put money on the table to have a fire camera network out there. We had not tested our emergency alert and warning system with the community to know if it worked or not. Our Emergency Operations Center was a bunker instead of a living connective nexus.

IN THE WAKE OF THE DISASTER, GORE RECRUITED VOLUNTEER BLOCK CAPTAINS TO ACT AS LIAISONS BETWEEN DAMAGED NEIGHBORHOODS AND POLICY MAKERS.

A week after the fire, we started having these big cacophonous town hall meetings. They devolved. People were leaving angrier than when they came. They couldn't get good, specific information. People who'd lost their homes had all this energy they didn't know what to do with.

I created the block captains as a network of people who I'd meet with every week, because it doesn't work to meet with a thousand people once a month. I needed a smaller group that was actionable and could give me ground truth. I needed ambassadors of recovery. For the next two years, they were the most powerful conduit for driving progress.

At the two-year anniversary, we hosted a group of the California State Association of Counties. All these block captains got up and spoke. They were shouting, "Wake up in your community!" They'd become powerful leaders. I was in awe.

When I became the chair, I made it our priority to build a recovery and resilience framework. We put money into emergency services. We tested our emergency alert systems. We created a Resilience Advisory Board at the California State Association of Counties and pushed that into the governor's office, and told everyone: this is the most important thing we have to do in our communities.

The key is not just to attain *higher* levels of preparedness, but to achieve *broader* levels of preparedness. "Higher" means the county and emergency management and our budget are up to the levels they should be, and we can say that now. But unless we have created a broad network or ecosystem of preparedness, nothing matters. It has to be a sinew that goes into every bit of what you do.

The idea of resilience is not that you never get hit. It's that when you do get hit, you can take it.

Are we ready for the next one? Yeah. Absolutely. There's never "good enough" in this. The movement toward "better" never ends. But we're ready to jump into action and respond. I have confidence in our systems. It kills me that we had to go through so much destruction to get there, but I can't control what went wrong. I can only control how we respond to it as a mandate to do better.

People talk about the "new normal" in the context of it being a horrible, apocalyptic, changing environment. I say that the "new normal" is how we rise to that challenge. The "new normal" is us. ■

171

FOR THE SECOND TIME IN TWO YEARS, KAREN AND I DROVE THIRTY-FIVE MILES SOUTH TO MOVE IN WITH OUR DAUGHTERS.

THEN THE NORTH WIND CAME, HOWLING OVER THE MOUNTAINTOPS AT MORE THAN 100 MILES PER HOUR, PUSHING THE KINCADE FIRE TO THE OUTSKIRTS OF GEYSERVILLE, HEALDSBURG, WINDSOR, AND NORTHERN SANTA ROSA.

Geyserville

Healdsburg

Windsor

Our Home

Kincade Fire (2019)

Tubbs Fire (2017)

Santa Rosa

Pacific Ocean

WORSE: EVERY COMPUTER MODEL TOLD FIREFIGHTERS THAT IF THE FIRE GOT PAST HIGHWAY 101, NOTHING WOULD STOP IT FROM BURNING THROUGH TWENTY MILES OF FIELDS AND FORESTED HILLS— INCLUDING MORE THAN 90,000 HOMES AND BUSINESSES—UNTIL IT HIT THE OCEAN.

US 101

ON SUNDAY, NEARLY 200,000 PEOPLE IN THE FIRE'S PROJECTED PATH WERE ORDERED TO LEAVE. KAREN'S JOB WAS TO SHELTER THOSE WHO HAD NOWHERE TO GO.

SONOMA COUNTY HAD LEARNED A LOT ABOUT CATASTROPHIC BLAZES IN THE PAST TWO YEARS. ONE OF SEVERAL NEW INFRARED CAMERAS ATOP AREA PEAKS SPOTTED THE KINCADE FIRE MINUTES AFTER IT BEGAN.

FIRST RESPONDERS WORKED TOGETHER LIKE NEVER BEFORE. MORE THAN 5,000 FIREFIGHTERS FROM AS FAR AS SOUTH DAKOTA ANSWERED OUR DISTRESS CALL.

THE FULL STORY OF FIREFIGHTERS' HEROISM WOULDN'T BE TOLD FOR WEEKS. THEY FULLY EXPECTED THE KINCADE FIRE TO JUMP THE FREEWAY AND RUN UNIMPEDED TO THE SEA.

BUT THEY FORMED LINES ALONG EVERY STREET WHERE WILDLANDS MET CITY, THEIR BACKS TO PEOPLE'S HOUSES AND THEIR HOSES AIMED INTO THE GLOWING WIND.

FIREFIGHTERS WHO'D FELT ENORMOUS GUILT FOR FAILING TO STOP THE 2017 FIRESTORMS SAID IT WAS THEIR SHOT AT REDEMPTION. THEY STOOD . . .

AND THEY HELD.

PG&E CUT POWER TO TWO MILLION NORTHERN CALIFORNIANS TO PREVENT MORE FIRES FROM DOWNED POWER LINES—A LEGACY OF ITS DECISION TO PAY MILLIONS IN EXECUTIVE BONUSES AND SHAREHOLDER DIVIDENDS INSTEAD OF MAINTAINING ITS GRID. KAREN AND I CAMPED IN OUR DAUGHTERS' APARTMENT IN THE DARK.

MISS SCARLET IN THE STUDY WITH A ROPE.

SUNDAY. MONDAY. TUESDAY.

EACH NIGHT THE WIND ROSE UP LIKE A RAGING DRAGON FROM THE NORTH, AND WE WONDERED IF THAT WAS THE NIGHT OUR HOUSE WOULD BURN DOWN AGAIN. I CHECKED THE FEED FROM OUR NEW VIDEO DOORBELL OBSESSIVELY.

IT'S STILL THERE!

THERE'S A NECESSARY POLICY DISCUSSION TO BE HAD ABOUT INDIVIDUAL RIGHTS VERSUS PUBLIC GOOD. MAYBE SOME PLACES ARE SO DANGEROUS THAT NO ONE SHOULD BE ALLOWED TO BUILD IN THEM.

AT THE SAME TIME, CLIMATE CHANGE IS INCREASING RISK IN A LOT OF PLACES THAT WERE NOT ESPECIALLY DANGEROUS BEFORE. IT'S A MOVING TARGET.

I DON'T KNOW THE ANSWER.

BY WEDNESDAY, IT WAS CLEAR THAT OUR NEIGHBORHOOD, AND ALL THE MAJOR CITIES IN SONOMA COUNTY, HAD BEEN SAVED. THIS TIME.

THE NEXT DAY WAS HALLOWEEN. WE WERE HOME.

ON THURSDAY, MY HOUSE DID **NOT** DISAPPEAR.

AFTERWORD

Karen and I evacuated our home north of Santa Rosa, California, at around 1:30 A.M. on Monday, October 9, 2017. Based on when our neighbors began getting text messages from their home security systems, we think our neighborhood burned around 2:30 A.M.

The first photo I shot as I walked back to the area later that morning is time-stamped 8:04 A.M. It took the firestorm less than six hours to scour a good-sized subdivision from the planet.

The next day, in addition to buying shoes and other necessities, I also bought the only art supplies I could find: a pad of low-quality pulp paper, one permanent marker, a fine-point felt-tip pen, and four colored highlighters. That afternoon, I began writing and drawing *A Fire Story*.

I've done journalism before, and *A Fire Story* felt like journalism to me. Someone called it my way of "bearing witness," and I couldn't put it better than that. I was there. I saw these extraordinary events. I had to tell what it was like the best way I knew how: in the form of a comic.

I drew the original eighteen pages of *A Fire Story* over parts of four days, and posted them online on October 13 and 15, 2017. They immediately went viral. News outlets picked up the story, and soon it had been featured on CNN, the *Washington Post, Entertainment Weekly, Mother Jones,* San Francisco newspapers and TV stations, and more.

To say my feelings about all that were conflicted is an understatement. Karen and I were dealing with a mind-numbing disaster while I was also hosting reporters and TV crews in our daughters' little apartment. There was no joy in the experience, but there was satisfaction in people reading our story and saying it helped them understand what it was like to be there. People who'd been through the fire with us said I got it right.

Around 700,000 people read the original comic on my blog, and another three million or so saw an animated version produced by San Francisco PBS station KQED that was picked up by National Public Radio (NPR). KQED producer Kelly Whalen came to my girls' place to record Karen and me reciting scripted lines from our own lives, which Farrin Abbott expertly animated and edited. KQED couldn't have been more sensitive and respectful, and I loved the short film they produced, which won a regional Emmy Award for Best Public/Current/Community Affairs-Feature/Segment on June 2, 2018.

I didn't write about my work on the original *Fire Story* webcomic, or the attention and commotion that went with it, in this book. Although this *Fire Story* is a graphic memoir, it isn't just *my* story; it's the story of thousands of people who lost everything, and hundreds of thousands who were affected less directly but still traumatically. Compared to the enormity of that universal experience, my particular unique situation was irrelevant.

The following pages are the original webcomic written and drawn in the few days immediately after the fire. My editor and I debated how to incorporate them into this book. They have a storytelling energy and urgency that comes from being created on the ground in the moment. But they're also a crude, slapdash record of me drawing as fast as I could with crummy materials on the worst days of my life.

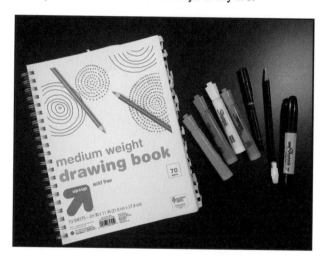

While I completely understand that the original story's spontaneity is part of what makes it worthwhile, I always considered it a rough first draft—part of the bigger story told in this book. I'm proud to include it here and happy I could take another crack at it.

I wish the fire hadn't happened. Since it did, I'm glad I was able to wring this small, good thing out of such a terrible disaster. I eventually laid to rest my ambivalence about telling *A Fire Story*. The way I see it, the fire owes me one.

My family is doing fine. As described in this expanded edition of *A Fire Story,* we rebuilt our house and moved in eighteen months after the original was destroyed. Now we're busy accumulating the days and nights and happy memories it takes to turn a house into a home.

ON MONDAY, MY HOUSE DISAPPEARED.

by Brian Fies *

AROUND ONE A.M., MY WIFE KAREN SNAPPED AWAKE. THE ELECTRICITY HAD GONE OUT.

I SMELL SMOKE.

CLOTHES I PACKED:

TWO PAIRS OF SOCKS (SHORT + LONG)
STRIPED T-SHIRT
SWEAT SHIRT
FLANNEL SHIRT
TOILETRY BAG
TWO TIGHTY-WHITEYS
PLUS THE JEANS, SHIRT, JACKET
    AND SANDALS I PUT ON.

STUFF WE GRABBED:

PHOTO ALBUMS
A FEW FRAMED PHOTOS + ART
ONE COPY OF EACH OF MY BOOKS,
    ENGLISH + FOREIGN (MISSED A FEW)
SOME JEWELRY
DRAWER OF IMPORTANT PAPERS.
COMPUTER BACKUP + USB DRIVES
DOG + CAT + THEIR STUFF
OUR DAUGHTERS' BEST STUFFED
    BUDDIES FROM INFANCY,
    BOO BEAR + PIGLET.

THAT'S JUST THE CALISTOGA FIRE. IT'S TWENTY MILES FROM HERE!

THE SKY IS GLOWING.

* But not to his usual standards.

ARE YOU GUYS O.K.?

YEAH, WE'RE GOING!

WRRRRRRRRRRRRR

EVACUATE NOW!

EVACUATE!

FIRE

COME ON! LET'S GO!

CALIFORNIA GEOLOGY RUNS NORTH AND SOUTH. NAPA AND SONOMA COUNTIES ARE SPLIT BY THE SMALL MAYACAMAS MOUNTAINS.

Calistoga

MY NEIGHBORHOOD LIES ALONG A CREEK THAT RUNS THROUGH THEM.

Napa

I AM HERE.

101

(Schulz Museum)

Santa Rosa

MONDAY NIGHT, A BLAZE THAT BEGAN 30 MILES AWAY NEAR CALISTOGA CAUGHT 50 MPH WINDS. A FLAMING FRONT SWEPT DOWN THE CREEK AND BROKE OVER THE HILLS LIKE A NAPALM TSUNAMI.

WE WERE AT THE TIP OF A BELLOWS FEEDING A BLAST FURNACE.

WE DIDN'T KNOW ANY OF THAT WHEN WE LEFT AT 1:30 A.M., FULLY EXPECTING TO RETURN VERY SOON. THE IDEA OF THAT DISTANT GLOW IN THE SKY ACTUALLY MAKING ITS WAY TO US WAS LUDICROUS.

WHERE SHOULD WE GO?

YOUR OFFICE.

KAREN IS DIRECTOR OF SONOMA COUNTY HUMAN SERVICES. HER OFFICE HAS A BACKUP GENERATOR, PHONES AND INTERNET, AND A SODA MACHINE. IT'S ALSO ONLY A FEW MILES FROM OUR HOUSE.

WE COULD HOLE UP THERE. BESIDES, IT WAS TIME FOR HER TO GET TO WORK.

BETWEEN 2 AND 7 A.M., KAREN ACTIVATED EMERGENCY PHONE TREES, ORGANIZED SHELTERS, AND PLANNED THE EVACUATION OF A FOSTER CHILDREN'S HOME AS FIRE BORE DOWN FROM THREE SIDE...

HOW MANY KIDS?

NO, YOU CAN'T GO WEST, THE HIGHWAY JUST CLOSED.

WHEN WILL THE COTS ARRIVE?

SHE WAS TOO BUSY TO THINK.

AT DAWN, I SET OUT TO GET AS CLOSE TO HOME AS I COULD.

DON'T DO ANYTHING STUPID.

WHO, ME?

THE SUN WAS A DIM ORANGE DISK IN A SALMON-GRAY CURTAIN OF SMOKE. I INHALED MY NEIGHBORS' LIVES.

I DROVE TO THE FIRST ROADBLOCK, PARKED IN A NEARBY LOT, AND STARTED WALKING.

KEPT WAITING FOR SOMEONE TO STOP ME BUT NO ONE DID.

TOOK THE SAME BACK STREETS WE'D DRIVEN OUT A FEW HOURS BEFORE.

THESE BLOCKS LOOKED ALL RIGHT! EVERYTHING WOULD BE JUST FINE!

THE STREET MADE A GENTLE CURVE INTO OUR NEIGHBORHOOD.

AS I ROUNDED IT, I **KNEW.**

FUCK.

fuck fuck fuck fuck fuck fuck fuck.

I PICKED MY WAY DOWN THE MIDDLE OF THE STREET TO AVOID SMOULDERING DEBRIS COLLAPSED INTO GUTTERS, ALONE ON A STERILE PLAIN.

BLACK TOOTHPICK TREES, MADLY TILTING CHIMNEYS, AND THE TWISTED STEEL FRAMES OF GARAGE DOORS.

HELL.

A FIREHOSE, SPLIT AND MELTED ON THE STREET, A VALIANT LAST STAND ROUTED INTO RETREAT.

A FALLEN HOOP THAT A BOY LOBBED BALLS AT FOR HOURS EVERY NIGHT AFTER DINNER.

THE STEEL POSTS OF MAILBOXES BENT LIKE HOT SUMMER TAFFY.

I TURNED ONTO MY STREET STUPIDLY HOPING TO SEE ANYTHING ELSE.

I USED TO HAVE FIVE REDWOOD TREES IN MY FRONT YARD.

I SEE A REFRIGERATOR AND THE ROUGH SHAPE OF A CAR I USED TO HAVE IN MY GARAGE.

I DON'T RECOGNIZE ANYTHING ELSE.

A TWO-STORY HOUSE FULL OF MY LIFE WAS A TWO-FOOT HEAP OF DEAD SMOKING ASH.

I CALLED KAREN AND TOLD HER SHE'D JUST BECOME ONE OF THE THOUSANDS OF REFUGEES SHE WAS HELPING.

HEY. I'M HERE. IN FRONT OF THE HOUSE.

BEGINNING THE LONG TRUDGE BACK, I PASSED A PRISTINE STARBUCKS ONLY A FEW HUNDRED YARDS FROM MY HOME.

STARBUCKS?!

HOW IS **THAT** FAIR?

I TRIED TO CALL A NEIGHBOR TO TELL HER, TOO, BUT RECEPTION WAS BAD AND I ENDED UP YELLING AT HER.

YOUR HOUSE IS GONE! IT'S ALL GONE!

NO, **GONE**!

IT WOULD HAVE ALMOST BEEN FUNNY IF I WEREN'T RUINING HER LIFE.

KAREN WAS A HERO THE REST OF THE DAY. WITH NINE-TENTHS OF HER STAFF OUT, SHE LED A TEAM THAT IMPROVISED AND PROBLEM-SOLVED. IT WAS IMPRESSIVE.

IN QUIET MOMENTS, WE INVENTORY LOST TREASURES, EACH A SWIFT STAB TO THE HEART. WE DIDN'T SAVE THE **WRONG** STUFF—WE WEREN'T THOSE PEOPLE WHO RISK THEIR LIVES FOR A JAR OF MUSTARD— WE JUST DIDN'T SAVE **ENOUGH** OF IT.

THINGS I WILL NEVER SEE AGAIN:

* MY GRANDMA'S DEPRESSION-GLASS CANDY JAR.
* MY GRANDPA'S WORLD WAR II FIELD CAP.
* OUR ANTIQUE PHONOGRAPH.
* CHILD-MADE ORNAMENTS.
* A TIME CAPSULE TO BE OPENED IN 2030.
* A SERIES OF PHOTOSTRIPS TAKEN BY CRAMMING OUR FAMILY INTO A BOOTH AT THE COUNTY FAIR EVERY SUMMER FOR 18 YEARS.
* MY MOM'S DIAMOND EARRINGS WE PLANNED TO RE-SET AND GIVE TO OUR GIRLS ON THEIR NEXT BIRTHDAY.
* EVERYTHING I EVER DREW OR PAINTED.

EVERYTHING ELSE.

WE CRASHED AT OUR DAUGHTERS' APARTMENT IN CLEARER AIR 30 MILES AWAY, TOO EXHAUSTED TO STAY AWAKE BUT TOO AMPED UP TO SLEEP.

ON TUESDAY I BOUGHT SHOES FOR WALKING AND BOOTS FOR DIGGING.

I SAW THINGS I'D NEEDED TWO DAYS EARLIER— FURNACE FILTERS, PRINTER INK, LIGHT BULBS— AND REALIZED I DIDN'T ANYMORE. IT'S UNNERVING TO NEED BOTH **EVERYTHING** AND **NOTHING**.

YOU CAN TELL AT A GLANCE IF A SHOPPER HAS LOST EVERYTHING THEY OWN.

UNDERWEAR, SOCKS, SHOES, WATER, TOOTHBRUSH AND PASTE, ONE LIGHT SHIRT, ONE HEAVY SHIRT.

YOU LOOK INTO THEIR CART. THEY LOOK INTO YOURS.

OCCASIONALLY IT SPARKS A CONVERSATION. USUALLY A NOD.

MY KEYRING HAS FIVE KEYS. THREE OF THEM DON'T DO ANYTHING ANYMORE.

Front door.

Mailbox melted on sidewalk.

Car incinerated in garage.

I WONDER HOW LONG IT'LL BE BEFORE I CAN BEAR TO TAKE THEM OFF.

KAREN AND I KNOW **DOZENS** BURNED OUT.

A FRIEND CARING FOR HIS HUSBAND WITH ALZHEIMER'S.

A RETIRED FBI AGENT WHO LOST A PRESENTATION FIREARM, AS WELL AS THE TICKETS AND POSTERS HIS DAUGHTER DREW WHEN SHE HELD A PRETEND CIRCUS IN THE BACKYARD 30 YEARS AGO.

A FAMILY WITH AN AUTISTIC SON WHOSE LIFE IS ANCHORED IN ROUTINE; THEY HAVEN'T TOLD HIM YET, HE THINKS THEY'RE ON VACATION.

THE WIDOW OF A FAMOUS CARTOONIST WHO LOST DECADES OF PRICELESS ARTWORK.

MARI ON THE CORNER, WHO CAN'T FIND HER CAT LUCY.

THOUSANDS OF HOMES HAVE BEEN DESTROYED IN THIS FIRESTORM. OURS WAS **ONE.**

The pages below were posted on October 31, 2017, after readers asked how we were doing.

A FEW WEEKS LATER...

I'M SELF-AWARE ENOUGH TO RECOGNIZE THE CLASSIC SYMPTOMS: SLEEPLESSNESS, LOSS OF APPETITE, MENTAL LAPSES, MOOD SWINGS.

SADLY, UNDERSTANDING TRAUMA DOESN'T REALLY HELP RELIEVE IT.

AFTER TWO WEEKS, WE WERE ALLOWED BACK TO OUR HOUSE. IT'S A FOOT-DEEP FOGBANK OF ASH.

ZZIP!

GLASS MELTED. CHINA FUSED. CONCRETE EXPLODED. STEEL TWISTED, ALUMINUM TRICKLED DOWN DRIVEWAYS.

MAYBE ONE DAY WE'LL APPRECIATE OUR FRESH START. NOT YET. NOT FOR A LONG LONG TIME.

WELL-MEANING PEOPLE SAY, "IT'S JUST STUFF," BUT IT WAS **OUR** STUFF.

STUFF WE CREATED, STUFF WE TREASURED, STUFF FROM OUR ANCESTORS WE WANTED OUR DESCENDANTS TO HAVE.

STUFF IS A MARKER OF TIME AND MEMORY.

IT'S **HOME.**

NOTES

Unless otherwise credited, all photos and artwork in *A Fire Story* are by the author, who mostly still draws with ink on paper.

Page 37: Photo copyright ©2017 Michael W. Harkins, used with permission and thanks.

Page 40: Satellite photo: NASA Earth Observatory image by Joshua Stevens, using MODIS data from LANCE/EOSDIS Rapid Response.

Large and small fires broke out all over the state during the night of October 8–9, 2017, due to a combination of sustained dry weather and unusually hot, strong winds blowing from the east. I consulted final incident reports produced by the California Department of Forestry and Fire Prevention (Cal Fire) to compile the following list of major fires (in order of area burned):

- Nuns Fire, Napa and Sonoma counties: 56,556 acres, 1,355 structures, 3 deaths
- Atlas Fire, Napa and Solano counties: 51,624 acres, 783 structures, 6 deaths
- Tubbs Fire, Napa and Sonoma counties: 36,807 acres, 5,636 structures (including my home), 22 deaths
- Redwood Valley Fire, Mendocino County: 36,523 acres, 546 structures, 9 deaths
- Pocket Fire, Sonoma County: 17,357 acres, 6 structures
- Cascade Fire, Yuba County: 9,989 acres, 264 structures, 4 deaths
- Cherokee Fire, Butte County: 8,417 acres, 6 structures
- LaPorte Fire, Butte County: 6,151 acres, 74 structures
- Sulphur Fire, Lake County: 2,207 acres, 150 structures
- Highway 37 Fire, Sonoma County: 1,660 acres, 30 structures
- Lobo Fire, Nevada County: 821 acres, 47 structures

Those fires account for the 8 counties, 8,900 structures, and 44 deaths mentioned in the text. In addition, the Bear Fire, which began in Santa Cruz County on October 16, 2017, burned 391 acres and destroyed 6 structures. An unrelated series of wildfires, the largest of them the Thomas Fire, struck southern California in early December 2017. In July and August 2018, the Mendocino Complex Fire, about forty miles north of Santa Rosa, burned more than 300,000 acres, which made it the largest wildfire in California history. Then, in November 2018, the Camp Fire near the northern California city of Chico destroyed approximately twice the number of homes, land, and lives as the 2017 firestorms that razed my home, succeeding it as the most destructive wildfire in California history.

These records should not be broken every fire season.

In late 2019 and early 2020, the entire continent of Australia suffered one of the most widespread and destructive wildfires in history. More than 20 million acres burned—fifteen times more land than was lost in the 2017 California fires combined—and more than a billion animals may have been killed, with some species facing extinction. Although the Australian bushfires were much larger than the fire that destroyed my home, the disasters had much in common: blazes that would not normally have been so destructive were amplified by years of drought and extraordinarily strong winds into unstoppable infernos.

Page 48: Information regarding the number and cost of U.S. disasters in 2017 is from the National Oceanic and Atmospheric Administration's (NOAA) National Centers for Environmental Information (ncdc.noaa.gov). In this context, a "major disaster" is one that was declared under the Stafford Disaster Relief and Emergency Assistance Act, which was invoked fifty-seven times in 2017, mostly due to fires and hurricanes.

In addition to assistance provided by the County of Sonoma, FEMA, and other government agencies, several organizations came forward to gather and distribute contributions:

- The Redwood Credit Union's North Bay Fire Relief Fund collected more than $32 million. Some of those dollars were used to meet fire victims' immediate food and housing needs, others were given as cash. My family received $2,000 from this fund. Redwood Credit Union stopped accepting donations for its Fire Relief Fund in February 2018.
- Tipping Point (tippingpoint.org/relief) raised more than $33 million, much of it through two high-profile "Band Together Bay Area" rock concerts. The group has been distributing the proceeds over time for fire relief, recovery, and rebuilding efforts. Much of their support has been given in the form of grants to local nonprofits and other organizations providing direct assistance.
- Community Foundation Sonoma County (sonomacf.org) established the Sonoma County Resilience Fund to address the area's mid- to long-term recovery. The Community Foundation is focusing its efforts on what it identifies as three key areas of greatest need: helping individuals impacted by the fires, healing the long-term effects of trauma, and finding housing solutions for the community.

If you're moved to help, I would recommend a contribution to the Sonoma County Resilience Fund.

Also, as mentioned on **page 51**, Creative Sonoma (creativesonoma.org), a program of the Sonoma County Economic Development Board, provided cash grants to artists—including me—to replace destroyed art equipment and supplies.

The Red Cross deployed quickly and provided funding for both short- and long-term needs. Many other public and private groups, too numerous to name, gave invaluable aid and support to fire victims in the days and months following the disaster. My thanks and appreciation to them all.

Page 168: On the night of October 23, 2019, the Kincade Fire started northeast of Geyserville, California in northern Sonoma County. Over the next week, according to Cal Fire, it burned 78,000 acres and destroyed 374 structures. As bad as it was, the Kincade Fire could have been much, much worse. The mass evacuation of 200,000 residents let firefighters concentrate on fighting the fire rather than rescuing citizens, and their heroism, combined with a great deal of luck, kept the Kincade Fire from entering cities and consuming half the county.

Page 178: Emmy photo by Karen Fies (June 2, 2018). XO.